The Best Test Preparation for the
CAHSEE

English-Language Arts

Daniel L. Moody, M.A.
School of Languages and Humanities
Southwestern College
Chula Vista, California

Edited by David Rosen, M.A.

Research & Education Association
61 Ethel Road West
Piscataway, New Jersey 08854

**THE BEST TEST PREPARATION FOR THE
CAHSEE: ENGLISH-LANGUAGE ARTS**

Printed in the United States of America

Library of Congress Control Number 2004117903

International Standard Book Number 0-7386-0001-6

REA® is a registered trademark of Research & Education Association, Inc.,
Piscataway, New Jersey 08854.

A05

ABOUT OUR AUTHOR

Daniel L. Moody is a Professor in the School of Languages and Humanities at Southwestern College in Chula Vista, California, where he teaches Grammar, Listening/Speaking, and Writing in the English as a Second Language program, as well as Basic Writing and Editing for both native English speakers and bilingual students.

He received a B.A. in French with a minor in Spanish from San Diego State University in 1984 and an M.A. in English as a Second Language from the University of Arizona in 1985. In the past ten years, he has coauthored several textbooks for developmental level college writing with Professor Anna Ingalls, including *Expectations: A Reader for Developing Writers*, now in its second edition.

The author wishes first to thank his wife, Kathleen, and their four daughters for their support of this project. He also owes a debt of gratitude to Professor Anna Ingalls for providing examples of good organization and great writing, and to his dean, Dr. Renée Kilmer, for originally calling this project to his attention. Finally, Allison Smith, Publications Consultant for the California Department of Education, ably and professionally facilitated permissions and information requests.

ABOUT OUR EDITOR

David Rosen received his B.A. and M.A. degrees from the University of Oregon. He is currently developing a comprehensive English program for a private preparatory high school in California. Mr. Rosen is listed in the "Who's Who Among America's Teachers" and is cited by several honor students as being their most influential instructor.

ABOUT RESEARCH & EDUCATION ASSOCIATION

Founded in 1959, Research & Education Association is dedicated to publishing the finest and most effective educational materials—including software, study guides, and test preps—for students in middle school, high school, college, graduate school, and beyond. Today, REA's wide-ranging catalog is a leading resource for teachers, students, and professionals. We invite you to visit us at www.REA.com to find out how "REA is making the world smarter."

ACKNOWLEDGMENTS

In addition to our author and editor, we would like to thank Larry B. Kling, Vice President, Editorial, for his editorial direction; Diane Goldschmidt, Associate Editor, and Teresina Jonkoski for their editorial contributions; Jeanne Audino, Senior Editor, for preflight editorial review; Jeff LoBalbo, Senior Graphic Designer, for providing pre-press electronic mapping; and Mike Cote for typesetting the manuscript. Supervising press readiness was Pam Weston, Vice President, Publishing.

CONTENTS

Chapter 7: Punctuation and Capitalization   147

Section 4: Essay Writing 175

PRACTICE TEST 1   225

PRACTICE TEST 2   291

CAHSEE
English-Language Arts

Section 1:

Introduction

Passing the CAHSEE: English-Language Arts

About this Book

This book will provide you with an accurate and complete representation of the English-Language Arts section of the California High School Exit Examination (CAHSEE). Inside you will find reviews that are designed to provide you with the information and strategies needed to do well on the test. Two practice tests are provided, both of which are based on the official CAHSEE. The practice tests contain every type of question that you can expect to encounter on the CAHSEE English-Language Arts. Following each test, you will find an answer key with detailed explanations designed to help you completely understand the test material.

About the Test

Who Takes the Test and What is it Used For?

Beginning with the class of 2006, every high school student who plans to graduate from a California public high school must first pass the California High School Exit Examination (CAHSEE). The test consists of two parts: Mathematics and English-Language Arts.

Students are first required to take the CAHSEE in grade 10. Those who pass both parts, Mathematics and English-Language Arts, have completed the test requirement for graduation and do not have to retake the test. Students who do not pass either or both parts need to retake the part or parts they have not passed in 11th grade and 12th grade, until they pass.

When and Where Is the Test Given?

Every public school district in California will provide students with multiple opportunities to take the CAHSEE. Each district may administer the CAHSEE several times a year, choosing from a list of test dates that are designated by the State Superintendent of Public Instruction.

The CAHSEE test is administered over two days. The English-Language Arts section is given on the first day followed by the Mathematics portion the next day.

Is There a Registration Fee?

No. Because all California public high school students are required to take and pass this test in order to receive a high school diploma, no fee is required.

Test Accommodations and Special Situations

Parents of special education students, students with disabilities (including attention deficit disorder), and students who are learning English should contact their local high school officials regarding possible waivers, extra time, or special arrangements (*accommodations* or *modifications*) during the CAHSEE. These special arrangements can include the use of a calculator, special seating, a quiet environment, or a large print test booklet, among others. English learners may be able to use a glossary.

Scoring of the test may be done differently, depending on whether the special arrangement is an accommodation or a modification. Ask your school officials for further information or check on the CAHSEE website.

Additional Information and Support

Additional resources to help you prepare to take the CAHSEE include:

• the official State of California CAHSEE website at http://www.cde.ca.gov/ta/tg/hs/resources.asp

• REA's *The Best Test Preparation for the CAHSEE Mathematics*

How to Use this Book

What Do I Study First?

Read over the review sections and the suggestions for test-taking. Studying the review sections thoroughly will reinforce the basic skills you need to do well on the test. Be sure to take the practice tests to become familiar with the format and procedures involved with taking the actual CAHSEE.

To best utilize your study time, follow our CAHSEE Independent Study Schedule located on page xix of this book.

When Should I Start Studying?

It is never too early to start studying for the CAHSEE. The earlier you begin, the more time you will have to sharpen your skills. Do not procrastinate! Cramming is *not* an effective way to study, since it does not allow you the time needed to learn the test material. The sooner you learn the format of the exam, the more time you will have to familiarize yourself with the exam content.

Format of the CAHSEE: English-Language Arts

Overview of the English Language Arts Portion of the CAHSEE

The English-Language Arts portion of the CAHSEE is designed to test students' ability to read and write, knowledge of basic literary concepts, and familiarity with basic writing strategies. Each exam has 72 multiple-choice questions and one essay. In addition, there are seven multiple-choice questions that are not scored; they are just being tried out for future tests.

Types of Questions

There are a total of 45 multiple-choice questions that test **reading** ability. These fall into the following categories:

- Word Analysis—7 Questions

- Reading Comprehension—18 Questions

- Literary Response and Analysis—20 Questions

There are a total of 27 multiple-choice questions that test **writing** ability. These questions are divided as follows:

- Writing Strategies—12 Questions

- Written English Language Conventions—15 Questions

Students must also write one essay, assigned at random from five possible essay types.

Scoring the Practice Tests

These practice tests cannot determine what exact score you would receive when taking the actual CAHSEE, but they can help you find out if you are improving. To pass the English-Language Arts portion of the CAHSEE you need to receive approximately 60% of the possible points.

To get a rough estimate of the percentage correct on each of the two practice tests in this book, follow this procedure:

1   Determine the approximate score (1 4) on the writing sample by asking several people to compare it with the sample essays in the "Detailed Explanations of Answers" section that follows each practice test.   _____

2.   Multiply by 4.5.   _____ × 4.5 = _____

This number shows the approximate number of points you would receive for the essay.

3.   Determine the number of correct answers on the rest of the test.   _____

4. Add the number of correct answers to the number of points for the essay to find the total points.

    _____ + _____ = _____

5. Divide the total points by 90 to get an approximate percentage of points correct.

    _____ / 90 = _____

Test-Taking Strategies

What to Do Before the Test

-   **Pay attention in class**.

-   **Carefully work through the review sections of this book**. Mark any topics that you find difficult so that you can focus on them while studying and get extra help if necessary.

-   **Take the practice tests and become familiar with the format of the CAHSEE**. When you are practicing, simulate the conditions under which you will be taking the actual test. Stay calm and pace yourself. After simulating the test only a couple of times, you will feel more confident, and this will boost your chances of doing well.

-   **Students who have difficulty concentrating or taking tests in general may have severe test anxiety**. Tell your parents, a teacher, a counselor, the school nurse, or a school psychologist well in advance of the test. They may be able to suggest some useful strategies to help you feel more relaxed so that you can do your best on the test.

What to Do During the Test

- **Read all of the possible answers**. Just because you think you have found the correct response, do not automatically assume that it is the best answer. Read through each answer choice to be sure that you are not making a mistake by jumping to conclusions.

- **Use the process of elimination**. Go through each answer to a question and eliminate as many of the answer choices as possible. By eliminating two answer choices, you will give yourself a better chance of getting the item correct since there will only be two choices left to choose from.

- **Work quickly and steadily and avoid focusing on any one question for too long**. Taking the practice tests in this book will help you learn to budget your time on the actual test.

- **Work on the easiest questions first**. If you find yourself working too long on one question, make a mark next to it on your test booklet and continue. After you have answered all of the questions that you know, go back to the ones that you skipped.

- **Be sure that the answer oval you are marking corresponds to the number of the question in the test booklet**. Since the multiple-choice sections are graded by machine, marking one wrong answer can throw off your answer key and your score. Be extremely careful.

- **Work from the answer choices**. You can use a multiple-choice format to your advantage by working backwards from the answer choices to answer the question. You may be able to make an educated guess based on eliminating choices that you know do not fit the question.

The Day of the Test

On the day of the test, you should wake up early after a decent night's rest and have a good breakfast. Make sure to dress comfortably, so that you are not distracted by being too hot or too cold while taking the test, and give yourself enough time to arrive at your school early. This will allow you to collect your thoughts and relax before the test.

CAHSEE INDEPENDENT STUDY SCHEDULE

The following study schedule allows for thorough preparation for the CAHSEE. If you are not enrolled in a structured course, be sure to set aside enough time—at least two hours each day—to study. But no matter which study schedule works best for you, the more time you spend studying, the more prepared and relaxed you will feel on the day of the exam.

Week	Activity
Week 1	Study Section 2. Be sure to thoroughly work through all the tasks and questions given. If you have particular trouble with any of them, go back and study the corresponding section of the review.
Week 2	Study Section 3. Again, be sure to complete all tasks and questions. If any particular type of question gives you trouble, review that section again.
Week 3	Study Section 4, and be sure to complete all tasks and questions. If any particular type of question gives you trouble, review that section again. Have two teachers check your work.
Week 4	Take Practice Test 1, and after scoring your exam, review carefully the explanations to the questions you missed. If there are any types of questions that are particularly difficult for you, review those subjects by studying the appropriate section again.
Week 5	Take Practice Test 2, and after scoring your exam, review carefully the explanations to the questions you missed. If there are any types of questions that are particularly difficult for you, review those subjects by studying the appropriate section again.

CAHSEE
English-Language Arts

Section 2:

Reading Skills

Vocabulary

You can expect to see seven vocabulary (Word Analysis) questions on the CAHSEE test. Increasing your vocabulary can help you raise your score on these vocabulary questions. Improving your vocabulary will also make other parts of the test easier, especially the reading comprehension questions.

In this chapter, you will learn several ways to improve your vocabulary in preparation for taking the CAHSEE. These include the following helpful topics:

- Vocabulary Development Tools

    — Using a Dictionary

    — Making a Word List

    — Practicing with Flashcards

- Root Words

- Understanding Vocabulary from Context

- Figurative Language

  — Idiomatic Expressions

  — Similes and Metaphors

- Synonyms and Antonyms

- Commonly Confused Words

Vocabulary Development Tools

One useful strategy that can improve your vocabulary and increase your score on the CAHSEE is to be sure that you understand the words you read. A dictionary, a word list, and flashcards are all useful tools for doing this.

Using a Dictionary

A dictionary is an important tool to improve your vocabulary. In fact, you should have access to two types of dictionaries: a paperback dictionary that you can carry with you to school, and a larger desk dictionary to use when you study in the library or at home. A desk dictionary has a larger number of words as well as more information about each word. If you have access to a computer, you can use a software or Internet dictionary.

If English is not your first language, you should also have a two-way bilingual dictionary (for example, Spanish-English/ English-Spanish or Vietnamese-English/English-Vietnamese).

There are two strategies that can help you use a dictionary effectively: *learn the parts of speech* and *learn related words.*

Learn the Parts of Speech

The first strategy is to learn the parts of speech and the dictionary abbreviations for them. For a complete list of the parts of speech, check the front pages of your dictionary.

Here is a list of symbols for the most common parts of speech:

adj.   adjective: a word that describes a noun

adv.   adverb: a word that describes an action verb (Some adverbs have other uses. For more detailed information on adjectives and adverbs, see Chapter 6.)

n.   noun: a person, place, thing, idea, or animal

pron. pronoun: a word that represents a noun

> *v.*   verb: a word that shows an action, a condition, or existence (also *v.i., v.t.,* or *vb* in some dictionaries).

Suppose you want to look up the meaning of the word *manifest* in the sentence, "The inspector checked the ship's manifest." The dictionary gives more than one meaning for the word *manifest.* The first meaning might be *obvious (adj.)* and the second meaning *a shipping list (n.).* The symbol *adj.* means *adjective*: a word that describes a noun. The symbol *n.* means *noun*: a person, place, thing, idea, or animal.

If you can figure out that in this sentence the word *manifest* is a thing of some kind, you will know that the correct definition is the second one, because it is marked *n.* for noun: *a shipping list.*

Sometimes, more than one meaning is given, and both meanings are the same part of speech—two nouns, for example. If this is the case, make an educated guess and later ask a teacher to be sure you understand the meaning of the word.

Learn Related Words

The second strategy for learning vocabulary with a dictionary is to learn the related words and expressions for each word you look up. For example, if you look up the word *passive,* you would probably find the words *passively* and *passivity* listed as well, and depending on the dictionary, possibly *passive resistance, passive role,* and *passive voice.* By taking a moment to learn these related forms and phrases, you will be adding depth and richness to your vocabulary.

Making a Word List

Another way to improve your vocabulary is to make a word list—a list of new or unfamiliar words that you come across in your readings or studies.

There are different ways to make a word list. One way is as follows: Use several pages in the back of your school notebook. Starting with the last page in your notebook, draw a vertical line down the left side of the page, about one-third of the way in. Then, every time you come across a new word, write the word on the left side of the line, and write the meaning of the word on the right side of the line (Look it up in a dictionary). Then, write an example sentence below the meaning. Later, you can review all of the new words by covering up either side of your word list with a piece of paper and quizzing yourself. Even better, practice with a partner or members of a study group.

Practicing with Flashcards

Flashcards can also help you memorize new vocabulary from your word list. You can buy blank flashcards or use three-by-five index cards, which are available at any drugstore or office supply store.

To make flashcards, write a new, unfamiliar, or difficult word on one side of the card, and the meaning on the other. Then, when you have collected a stack of flashcards, divide them into two smaller stacks, depending on how well you know the words.

To do this, go through the list, asking yourself the meaning of each word. Put the ones that you get right into the "easy" stack and the ones that you get wrong into the "need to learn" stack.

After you have reviewed all of the flashcards, go through the "easy" stack two more times. If you miss any of these words, put them in the other stack.

The words that are left in the "easy" stack go into a stack that you only review once in a while, but the stack with the words that you missed should be reviewed every day, until you know them very well.

By spending 10 or 15 minutes a day reviewing the words on your flashcards, you can improve your score on the vocabulary questions of the CAHSEE.

Root Words

Root words are the basic building blocks of meaning in many words. They occur in many words and have the same meaning in each one. By learning a relatively small number of root words, you will be able to understand many words that contain the same roots.

For example, if you know that EX means *out* and PATRIA means *fatherland* or *country*, you should be able to puzzle out that an *expatriate* has something to do with being out of the country. If you choose the answer that an *expatriate* is a person who is living outside of his or her home country, you will have answered that vocabulary question correctly—even though you may never have seen the word *expatriate* before!

By learning the roots *ex* and *patria*, you will have a good idea of the meanings of any words that contain either of these two root words. Two more examples are *exterminate* (to wipe out or end completely) and *repatriate* (to send something back to the country it came from).

Example:

The police *repatriated* the stolen Mayan artifacts.

By memorizing the commonly used root words in this section, you will have a useful tool to help you answer some of the vocabulary questions on the CAHSEE.

Common Root Words

Root Word	Meaning of Root	Example with Definition	Other Examples
A, AN	not, without	amoral (without a sense of morality)	apolitical, asymmetrical, atheist
AD, AF, AT	to	adhere (to stick to)	affix, attract, attach
AMBI, AMPHI	both	ambidextrous (able to use both hands equally)	ambiguous, ambivalent, amphibian
ANN, ENN	year	annual (yearly)	anniversary, annuity, centennial
ANTE, ANTI	before	antecedent (something that came before)	anticipate, antediluvian, antiquarian
ANTHRO, ANDRO	man	android (a man-like robot)	anthropologist, misanthrope, philanthropist
ANTI	against	antibiotic (a medicine that kills germs)	antidote, antifreeze
APO	away	apology (taking back one's words or actions)	apogee
ARCH, ARCHE, ARCHI	main	archenemy (main enemy)	architect

Common Root Words (continued)

Root Word	Meaning of Root	Example with Definition	Other Examples
AUTO	self	autocratic (dictatorial: where one person makes the rules)	automatic, autonomous
BEN, BENE	good, well	beneficial (helpful)	benefactor
BI	two	bicycle (having two wheels)	bifocals, binational
BIO	life	the study of life	antibiotic, biosphere
CHRON	time	chronological (organized by time order)	chronometer, chronic
CIRCUM	around	circumference (the distance around a circle)	circumnavigate, circumstantial
CO, COM, CON	with	coworkers (people who work together)	communicate, connection
CRAT, -CRACY	govern	democracy (government by the people)	autocrat, meritocracy
CRED	believe	incredible (unbelievable)	credit, credibility
DEM	people	demographics (information about the people in general)	demagogue, democracy
DICT	speak	benediction (a spoken blessing)	dictionary, prediction
DIS, DI	un-	disengage (to pull back from)	distrust, disobey
EQU	equal	equilateral (having two equal sides)	equivalent, equation
EU	good	euphonious (having a good sound)	euphemism
EX	out (*or* former)	exhale (to breathe out)	exile, exclusion
FID	faith	fidelity (faithfulness)	confident, fiduciary
GRAPH, GRAM	writing	telegram (a message sent from a far distance)	autograph, anagram
IN, IM, IR, IL	not	impossible (not possible)	irresponsible, insensitive, illegible
LOG, -LOGY	word (*or* the study of)	travelogue (a story about travel)	theology, biologist
LOCU, LOQU	speech, speak	loquacious (talkative)	locution, interlocutor

Common Root Words (continued)

Root Word	Meaning of Root	Example with Definition	Other Examples
MAL	bad	maladjusted (badly adjusted)	malady, malodorous
METER	measurement	chronometer (an instrument that measures time, such as a clock)	speedometer, metric
MIS	wrong	misprint (to write something wrong)	mistaken, misunderstand
MISS, MIT	send	transmit (to send across)	mission, remit
MONO	one	monotone (in one tone of voice)	monorail, monologue
NOM, NYM	name	synonym (another name for the same thing)	pseudonym, nominal, nominate
PAN	every	panacea (a remedy for everything)	Pan-American
PATH	feeling (*or* disease)	sympathetic (sharing the same feelings)	sociopath, empathy
PED	child	pediatrician (a doctor whose specialty is children)	pedagogy
PED, POD	foot	podiatrist (a doctor whose specialty is foot)	pedestal, podium
PHIL, PHILE	love	philanthropist (someone who loves to help people)	philosophy, bibliophile
PHOB	fear	arachnophobe (someone who is extremely afraid of spiders)	phobia, agoraphobic
PHON	sound	telephone (a device that sends sounds from far away)	phonetic
POP	people	popular (liked by the people)	population
POST	after	postgraduate (a student who continues to study after graduation from college)	postdate, posterior
PRE	before	predict (to foretell the future)	prelude, premature
PRO	for, in favor of	pro and con (for and against)	proponent, prolife
QUAD	four	quadrilateral (having four sides)	quadratic
RE	again	rewrite (to write something over)	repeat, replay
SCRIB, SCRIPT	write	scribble (to write quickly)	scripture, scripted
SPEC, SPECT	see	spectacle (something worth seeing)	speculation, inspect

Common Root Words (continued)

Root Word	Meaning of Root	Example with Definition	Other Examples
SUB	below	subpar (below normal)	subordinate, submarine
SUPER	above or better	superior (better)	supervisor, supermarket
SYN, SYM	with	symbiotic (depending on each other)	syndrome, synthesis, symposium
TELE	far	television (seeing something from far away)	telephone, teleportation, telegram
TRANS	across	transportation (moving something)	transmit, transparent
TRI	three	triangle (a figure having three angles)	tricycle, trilateral
UN	not, opposite	unusual (not usual)	unbelievable, unlikely, unravel
UNI	one	unilateral (one-sided)	unicorn, uniform, unified
VIA	by way of	deviate (to detour from the straight path)	obvious
VOC, VOK	voice	vocalist (a singer)	vociferous

Example Question:

What is the meaning of *triumvirate* in this sentence?

Caesar originally governed Rome as part of a triumvirate, an arrangement which he eventually repudiated.

A   committee of two people

B   committee of three people

C   committee of five people

D   committee of elderly people

The prefix *tri-* means *three*, so B is the best answer.

Understanding Vocabulary from Context

When you come across a word that you do not recognize, it is often possible to guess the meaning of the word from the <u>context</u>. The term *context* means the other information in the reading: nearby words, sentences, or paragraphs.

Sometimes a clue or even the exact definition of the unfamiliar word is given in the reading, as in the following sentence:

- I attended a lecture on sublacustrian geological formations, rock structures that lie underneath a lake.

The context of the word *sublacustrian* includes the rest of the sentence, which tells us that sublacustrian means *underneath a lake*.

Other times there is a dash, parentheses, or commas to set off the example or definition. Here are some more examples using commas, parentheses, and dashes:

- Pyrite, a yellow metal also known as fool's gold, is found in the region.

- Potassium chloride (a substitute for common table salt) can be obtained at any supermarket.

- In antediluvian times—before the great flood—the climate of the Mediterranean basin was completely different.

Even when the specific definition is not given in the sentence, paying attention to the *context* can help you make an educated guess about the meaning. This is important in test situations such as the CAHSEE, where you cannot use a dictionary.

Example Question:

What does the word *ballooned* mean in this sentence:

The number of students attending community colleges has ballooned to a new high in the past year.

A   celebrated

B   increased

C   decreased

D   cost

The words "to a new high" in this context give the idea that the word *ballooned* means *to rise or be increased*. The correct answer is B.

Figurative Language

Sometimes a sentence includes a word or expression that does not mean exactly what it says. These expressions are examples of *figurative language,* and can be any of the following three types:

- Idiomatic Expressions (or *Idioms*)

- Similes

- Metaphors

Idiomatic Expressions

An idiomatic expression, or *idiom*, is a phrase (a group of words) that has a different meaning from the individual words it contains. For example, the idiom *to get to the bottom of something* means to find out the complete truth—not to literally find the bottom of something.

Another example of an idiom is *Drop everything!* This idiomatic expression means to stop whatever you are doing so that you can pay attention to something else—it doesn't mean to literally drop whatever you are holding.

If you are learning English, you may not be familiar with some of the idioms on the CAHSEE. English has many idioms, but you can become familiar with many of them at several online websites on the Internet. Several online idiom sites are listed at http://www.usingenglish.com/links/Idiomatic_Expressions/.

A dictionary of idioms such as the *American Heritage®️ Dictionary of Idioms* can also be very helpful.

Similes and Metaphors

Metaphors and *similes* are techniques that writers use to make their writing more descriptive. They help the reader visualize similarities between different or unrelated things.

Metaphors

Metaphors say that something **is** something else, even though not in a literal sense. "I rested in the secure harbor of my bedroom" is a metaphor, because it states that my bedroom **is** a safe harbor. This metaphor communicates the idea that my bedroom feels like a safe and protected place.

"Our stay at the mountain cabin was a little slice of heaven" is another example of a metaphor. Of course, the mountain cabin wasn't really in heaven, but being there was so wonderful that the writer used *heaven* as a metaphor for the great time he spent there.

Similes

While a *metaphor* tells us that something **is** something else, a *simile* states that something **is like** something else, and often contains one of the following words: ***like***, ***as***, ***similar***, the ***same***. Like metaphors, similes show that something is similar to something else, especially something that might be surprising. For example, the following sentence contains a simile that compares a person to an apple pie:

- George's grandma is *as warm and sweet as the apple pie* she bakes from the apples that grow in their own small orchard.

"I felt *like a soaring eagle* in my new treehouse" is another simile. So is "The snowflakes blew around us *like millions of pieces of microwaved popcorn.*"

The CAHSEE tests to see that you understand the *meaning* of figurative language. You may also be asked to identify which answer is an example of an *idiom*, a *simile*, a *metaphor*, or of figurative language in general, as in the following examples.

Example Question 1:

What does the expression *got a kick out of* mean in the following sentence?

The tour boat passengers *got a kick out of* seeing several dolphins leap out of the water.

A   were afraid of

B   were startled by

C   enjoyed

D   were injured by

Even though the words say "kick," of course no one really got kicked. The expression *to get a kick out of something* means to *enjoy* it. This is an example of an idiom. C is the correct answer.

Example Question 2:

Read the following sentence.

His outlook on life was the rock upon which the rest of the village depended.

Which answer in the sentence best describes the old man's personality?

A   silly

B   worried

C   aggressive

D   steady

Of course his personality was not really a rock! But by using this metaphor, the author gives the impression that the old man has a personality that is as solid and dependable as a rock. D, *steady*, is the best answer to this question.

Example Question 3:

Which of the following sentences contains an example of a simile?

A   My future was as bright as sunshine reflecting off a mirror.

B   The wind bent the trees double.

C   The noise of the waves echoed through the sea cave.

D   She observed the newly opened daffodils after the first rains.

Remember that similes contain words that mean *similar*, such as the word *as,* used twice in A above. A is the correct answer.

Example Question 4:

Which of the following sentences is an example of figurative language?

A   Our team finally scored late in the fourth quarter, after many fans had left in disgust.

B   The small platform in the tree was a pirate ship that took us on many a glorious adventure.

C   The book was already opened to the page where we had left off reading the night before.

D   Mild winters are normal in Southern California, but local mountain areas do receive some snow.

Answer B is the correct answer. The small treehouse is said to be a pirate ship in this metaphor.

Synonyms and Antonyms

Sometimes the CAHSEE test might ask you to identify a word or expression that means the same thing as another word: a *synonym*. It is important to identify the word that has the closest meaning to the original.

Other questions may ask for the word or expression with the *opposite* meaning, an antonym. Be sure to read each question carefully to see if the question is asking for a *similar* meaning or the *opposite* meaning.

Example Question 1:

What does *advisable* mean in the following sentence?

Watching a movie that has been previewed by a friend is advisable; however, do not be surprised if your tastes run in different directions.

A   believable

B   unfriendly

C   strange

D   recommended

This sentence is asking for a *similar* meaning. The best answer is D because the meaning of *recommended* is similar to *advisable*.

Example Question 2:

Read the following sentence:

Tadiyuki and Patricia did a thorough job of editing their essays before they turned them in.

Which of the following does NOT have the same meaning as the preceding sentence?

A   They did a complete and careful job of checking their essays before they turned them in.

B   They briefly looked over their essays before they turned them in.

C   They checked everything in the essays before they turned them in.

D   They did not overlook anything when they checked their essays before turning them in.

This question is asking for a *different* meaning from the original sentence, so B is the best answer.

Be sure that you read the directions carefully and understand whether the question is asking for the same meaning or the opposite meaning.

Commonly Confused Words

Certain words in English are confusing because they are very similar to other words. Memorizing the following list of words and definitions will help you answer questions about commonly confused words on the CAHSEE.

Commonly Confused Words

Word	Definition	Example
accept	to take something that is offered	He would not accept pay for helping carry the groceries.
except	everything but, everyone but	She finished all of her homework except French before dinner.
advice	a noun: recommendation(s)	They accepted their counselor's advice.
advise	a verb: to provide counsel	The counselor advised them to take a math class.
affect	usually a verb: to influence	The ocean affects our weather patterns.
effect	usually a noun: result	The ocean has an effect on our weather patterns.
beside	next to	The bus stopped beside the school.
besides	in addition	Besides sports, my favorite activity is eating.

Commonly Confused Words (continued)

Word	Definition	Example
complement	to go well with	Peanut butter and jelly complement each other.
compliment	noun or verb: to say something nice	I complimented her on her diligent homework habits.
conscience	the sense of right or wrong	His conscience was clean.
conscious	aware	We were not conscious of how late it was.
farther	more distant physically	She ran farther than I did.
further	additional, continued	This assignment requires further study.
it's	contraction of "it is" or "it has"	It's time to go. It's been fun.
its	possessive pronoun	The school won its fourth trophy this year.
precede	to go before	Two errors preceded our baseball team's loss.
proceed	to begin or continue	The game will proceed as soon as the rain stops.
quiet	not noisy	The library is a quiet zone.
quite	very, fairly, completely	The lecture was not quite finished when the bell rang.
than	a comparative	Our team made more baskets than our opponents.
then	next or after	First we went shopping; then we went to the beach.
their	belonging to them	Their house is on Bancroft Street.
there	a location at a distance	The book is over there on the table.
they're	contraction of "they are"	They're tired of writing essays.
to	toward or until	It was ten minutes to three o'clock.
too	excessively	That's too bad.
two	the number 2	I have two aunts who live nearby.

Directions: Choose the word or phrase that works best in the blank.

Example Question 1.

Jalapeño peppers really _____ me.

A effect

B affects

C effects

D affect

This sentence needs a *verb* that agrees with the subject *Jalapeño peppers*, so the best answer is D. A and C are usually nouns, and B does not agree with the subject. (For more information on subject and verb agreement, see Chapter 6.)

Example Question 2.

Almost all colleges offer many activities _____ just academic courses.

A then

B than

C beside

D besides

Answer A means *next* or *afterwards*, Answer B is used with *comparative adjectives* with *-er* or *more*, Answer C means *next to*, and Answer D means *in addition to*. D is the only answer with a meaning that makes sense in this sentence.

Reading Comprehension

There are 18 reading comprehension questions on the CAHSEE. These questions test for various reading skills that are reviewed in this chapter.

General Strategies

These important tips can help you improve your reading in general and raise your reading comprehension score on the CAHSEE.

- Schedule Time to Read

- Keep a Reading List and a Reading Log

Schedule Time to Read

Just as a professional athlete must schedule time to practice his or her sport, the best way to become a better reader is to read, read, and read some more. If you can schedule an extra hour each day just to read, your reading ability will probably improve dramatically.

You should read a mixture of school-related materials and readings that you find especially interesting. At least half of the reading you do should be fairly easy to understand without a dictionary, and the other half should have several unfamiliar vocabulary words or difficult expressions. This way, you will get enough practice with the easier materials, and you will learn some new words from the more difficult readings.

Keep a Reading List and a Reading Log

Another tip for improving your general reading ability is to keep a reading list and a reading log. You might want to write READING LOG at the top of a piece of paper in the back of your notebook, and READING LIST at the top of another piece of paper.

Reading List

A *reading list* is a page where you write down the names of articles, books, websites, and other material that you might want to read. For example, when someone tells you about a good book, an interesting magazine article, or a great website, you can quickly write down the name of the book, the title and date of the magazine, or the Internet address of the website in the back of your notebook. Then, when you have time, you can go to a library or search online for the titles on your reading list.

Reading Log

A *reading log* is a record of everything you read. Write the title, the author, where you found the material, and the main idea of the reading, plus any information that is interesting to you. Use anywhere from two lines to a half page for each reading log entry. In addition to making it easier for you to find good reading material, keeping a log of your reading will give you practice with an important reading skill: finding the main idea.

Specific Reading Skills

Most of the reading comprehension questions on the CAHSEE test for specific reading skills. Learning and practicing the following skills can make you a much better reader.

- Identifying the theme or main idea of a reading

- Selecting the best summary of a reading

- Discovering the meaning of an unfamiliar word from the other words around it (the *context*)

- Understanding connotations

- Finding important information rapidly by *skimming and scanning.*

The following reading selection will be used for several of the example questions in this chapter.

Reading Selection for Example Questions:

_____

How to Write a Paragraph

Have you ever sat down to write a paragraph in class or for homework, but your mind went absolutely blank? The four main steps that follow, *prewriting*, *writing*, *rewriting*, and *editing*, will help you write a good paragraph whenever you need to.

The first step is *prewriting*, which includes anything you do to get ideas and help organize your paper before you write. Some examples of prewriting are talking about your ideas with somebody else, *brainstorming*, or *freewriting*.

Talking about something before you write can be very helpful. You might want to form a study group with other students, or just talk to a friend or someone in your family who writes well. *Brainstorming* means writing down anything that comes into your mind, whether it's an idea for your topic or any little detail. *Brainstorming* doesn't have to be in any particular style, and what you write doesn't have to be in complete sentences. Just write down anything, anywhere on the paper, and organize it later. *Freewriting* means just writing sentences one after another, as fast as ideas come into your mind, again, without worrying about corrections.

The second step is *writing* your paper. Make sure that you have a topic sentence that tells the reader what the paper is about, interesting details and specific language, a logical order, and transitions that help the reader understand how your paragraph is organized. Also, include a conclusion that makes the paragraph feel finished.

Next is *rewriting*, also called *revising*, which means reading your paper over carefully to be sure that it is clear and conveys the message that you want it to say. Rewrite anything that is not clear, fill in any gaps, and in general do what it takes to make your wording effective.

Finally, *editing* (also called *proofreading*) is the last step before you turn in your paper. Now is the time to correct any mistakes in sentence structure, grammar, spelling, or punctuation.

By following these steps, you will increase your chances of communicating what you wish to say and of getting a good grade on your paragraph.

Identifying the Theme or Main Idea

One common type of question asks you to find the *theme*, also called the *main idea*, which is the most important idea that the writer of the reading wants to communicate to the reader.

In many reading selections, there is a *thesis statement* or *topic sentence* that states the main idea—what the paragraph or reading is about. To find the main idea, check the first two sentences of the reading first and see if there is one statement that tells you the topic and main point for the whole reading. If the first sentences don't contain the main idea, check the final two sentences, then the middle of the reading. Make sure that the sentence you choose applies to the whole reading.

Sometimes the main idea is not stated directly, especially in stories. If you don't find the main idea in the reading, just ask yourself what the reading is all about. Decide what the general topic is, and then ask yourself what the reading says about that topic.

- What is this reading about? (the general topic)

- What does the reading say about the general topic?

- What meaning does this story have for me?

Example Question:

(Refer back to the essay "How to Write a Paragraph" on pages 30-31.)

This essay includes instructions about how to write a good paragraph. Read the essay and answer the following question:

Which answer BEST describes the main idea of this essay?

A   Prewriting includes anything you do to get your ideas down on paper and organize them.

B   Writing a good paragraph is not easy.

C   Following these steps will help you write a good paragraph.

D   It is important to write good paragraphs in order to do well in high school.

The best answer is C, because the whole essay is about the steps needed to write a good paragraph.

Note: Questions about the main idea might use the words *theme* or *main idea*, or just ask *what the essay is about* or *what happens in a story*. You should answer all of these questions by identifying the main idea.

Selecting the Best Summary

You may be asked to identify which answer best *summarizes* an essay or part of a reading. Unlike the main idea, a summary must include all of the most important information from the reading selection. A summary might also contain a very few specific details, but usually it will not contain any.

Example Question:

(Refer back to the essay "How to Write a Paragraph" on pages 30-31.)

Which answer is the best summary of how to write a paragraph?

A   Prewrite, write, revise, and edit.

B   Brainstorm, freewrite, use transitions, and check for mistakes.

C   Follow these steps to write a good paragraph.

D   Prewrite; then write the introduction, body, and conclusion.

The essay states that the main steps are prewriting, writing, revising, and editing. The best answer is A.

Answer B is not correct because it includes some details along with the main steps. Answer C is the main idea. It is so short that it does not include the major points, and Answer D only mentions one important step and then switches to details about the body of the paper.

Discovering Meaning from Context

You may not understand every word in a certain reading, but don't let that stop you! You can usually figure out the basic meaning of the reading from other information in the reading that you do understand.

Review **Understanding Vocabulary from Context** in Chapter 1 for more information about understanding the meaning of words from the context.

Understanding Connotations

The *connotation* of a word or expression means the *feeling* or *shade of meaning*, separate from the literal meaning. For example, the word *aggressive* has a negative connotation in the following sentence:

Example Question 1:

The *aggressive* customer insisted on returning the broken merchandise.

The word *aggressive* in the preceding sentence gives the idea that the customer is acting:

A inappropriately

B strangely

C normally

D appropriately

The best answer is A, because the word aggressive has a feeling of *anger* or *pushiness* associated with it that is not appropriate in a business situation.

In the following sentence, the word *assertive* gives the same basic meaning, but without the negative feeling, or connotation:

- The *assertive* customer insisted on returning the broken merchandise.

Sometimes the CAHSEE will ask you about the feeling that certain words communicate to the reader.

Example Question 2:

What feeling do the following words communicate?

strolling, sunbathing, taking a nap

A energy

B rest

C organization

D friendship

The best answer is B, because all of these activities are restful.

Finding Information by Skimming and Scanning

Skimming and scanning is a quick way to find information in a reading. This technique will save you time when you answer some of the reading comprehension questions on the CAHSEE. The steps to skimming and scanning are:

1.   Be sure that you know what information you are looking for.

2.   Take a quick look at the whole reading, including graphs or charts, headings, anything in bold print, and of course the title. Look for key words and phrases.

3.   Read certain sections quickly: the introduction, the first line of each paragraph, the conclusion, and any subheadings.

4.   If you still haven't found the information you are looking for, try skimming each paragraph to pick out the key words that you are looking for. You may find the information there.

Skimming and scanning can help you answer questions like the following.

Example Question 1:

(Refer back to the essay "How to Write a Paragraph" on pages 30-31.)

What topic does this reading give the most information about?

A   prewriting

B   writing

C   revising and editing

D   writing the conclusion

The best answer is A because prewriting is the largest section of the essay.

Example Question 2:

What topic does this essay give the least information about?

A   revising and editing

B   writing

C   prewriting

D   sentence structure

The best answer is D. Sentence structure is only mentioned as a detail.

Example Question 3:

Which topic is not included in this essay?

A   transitions

B   editing

C   overcoming writer's block

D   writing a conclusion

The best answer is C. Writer's block was not mentioned in the essay.

Analysis of Readings

Some of the questions on the CAHSEE will require you to analyze a reading selection for the following points:

- The Purpose of a Reading

- Attitude, Tone, and Mood

- Plot, Conflict, and Resolution

- A Character's Personality, Feelings, and Relationships

- Literary Devices (Techniques and Strategies)

- Types of Literature (Genres)

- Supporting Information

- Unity

Analyzing the Purpose of a Reading (or Author's Purpose)

Writers have different purposes for the different things that they write. Some passages are written to give the reader information. A particular reading might include informational material, instructions for how to do something, or both. Other selections are written to convince or persuade the reader, and sometimes, the author just wants to entertain the reader.

Each version of the CAHSEE includes several questions that ask you to analyze the *purpose* of different kinds of readings. The purposes of the reading selections on the CAHSEE may include the following:

- To Inform

- To Persuade

- To Entertain

Recognizing the author's purpose can also help you understand the material in the reading, including the main idea and key points.

Wording of CAHSEE Questions and Answers

Some questions ask for the *purpose of the reading*, while others ask for the *author's purpose* or the *narrator's purpose*, which are just different ways of saying the same thing. Also, some questions will have the following words instead of the word *reading*: *selection*, *story*, *brochure*, *passage*, *document*, or *essay*. Even though the CAHSEE asks this type of question in many ways, the word <u>purpose</u> always appears in the question.

The following examples are similar to the questions and answers you will see on the CAHSEE test. The exact wording of each question and answer will be slightly different, so it is important to become familiar with the different questions and answers that you might find on the test.

Possible Questions:

- **What is the purpose of this reading?**

- **What is the main purpose of this reading?**

- **What is the narrator's purpose in writing this selection?**

- **The main purpose of this document is—**

- **What is the author's purpose in this passage?**

- **What is the author's main purpose in this story?**

Possible Answers:

To Inform:

- to present factual information

- to give an explanation

- to show or explain something

- to tell how to do something

- to explain how to do something

To Persuade:

- to convince or persuade

- to express an opinion

To Entertain:

- to entertain

Example Question:

What is the main purpose of the reading "How to Write a Paragraph"? (Refer back to the essay on pages 30-31.)

A   to show how good writers organize their day

B   to convince people that good writers are born that way

C   to show readers how to write well

D   to convince readers that writing good paragraphs is important

Everything in the paper is written to inform the reader how to write a good paragraph. The best answer is C.

Analyzing Attitude, Tone, and Mood

Many times, authors may express certain feelings about their topic or about some of the information that they write about. If you can notice and understand the writer's feelings and attitude toward the topic, you will often have a better idea of the author's message. Words used to describe how the author expresses his or her feelings include the words *attitude*, *tone*, and *mood*.

Author's Attitude

The author's *attitude* shows <u>approval</u> or <u>disapproval</u> of a particular point or even of the whole topic. A careful reader can usually decide if an author approves of a point by the clues provided in the written material.

The following example question will give you an idea of the type of question that you can expect about the author's attitude.

Read the following paragraph about backpacking.

Hiking and camping can be two of the most revitalizing and refreshing experiences that people can have. Overnight backpacking combines both of these, because backpackers have to carry everything they need on their backs, including food, cooking stoves and implements, a tent, clothing, first aid materials, and more. Unlike car camping, backpacking offers both a physical workout and the satisfying experience of getting in touch with nature far from highways and crowded public campgrounds.

Example Question:

Which of the following shows the writer's attitude toward overnight backpacking?

A   It is not appropriate for most people.

B   It is best to hike in groups of at least three people.

C   It can be dangerous.

D   It refreshes the body and the spirit.

The author refers to both physical exertion and getting in touch with nature. D is the best answer because it refers to both the body and the spirit.

Mood and Tone

Mood and *tone* are terms that are used to describe the *emotions* that the author communicates in a reading selection and the *manner* in which he or she communicates them to the reader.

Questions about *mood* are asking what emotions the writer seems to feel, while questions about *tone* are asking how the writing is supposed to feel to the reader. Questions about mood and tone are often very similar to each other.

Learning to identify the *mood* of a writing selection can help you catch things that the writer doesn't say directly, and to discover if the writer is treating the topic fairly, or with a bias.

Mood

Language used to describe *mood* includes any words that show feelings or emotions. These emotions can range from depressed to very happy, from angry to loving, from serious to silly, or any other emotions that the writer might be feeling or trying to communicate.

Most of the time the author does not come out and say what he or she feels, or how the writing is supposed to affect the reader. As a result, the best way to analyze the mood of a reading selection is to look for clues about how the author might be feeling about the topic. Look for interesting words and expressions that show the personality of the writer, and then ask yourself what mood the writer appears to be in.

For example, does it seem like the writer wants you to feel angry about something in the writing, or sad, or happy? Does the author seem to be sarcastic, approving, impressed, worried? Does the writer seem to want the reader to approve or disapprove of something, to appreciate something, or to be impressed by something in the selection? These are all clues to discovering the mood of the writer.

Tone

The *tone* of a reading is how the reading selection and its style feels to the reader. The tone may also reflect the *purpose* of the reading, or the *mood* of the author. Many of the words used to describe tone are similar to those used to describe mood, as listed below.

Mood and Tone Words

Many of the following words have been used on previous versions of the CAHSEE to describe *mood* and *tone*. Try to make sure that you understand all of these words before you take the test.

Mood and Tone Words

Mood or Tone Word	Definition	Similar Words
accepting	not judgmental	acceptance, accepted
amazed	very surprised	amazing, amazement
amusing	funny	amused, amusement
angry	mad	anger
anxious	worried	anxiety
awe	wonder and amazement	awed
bewildering	confusing or puzzling	bewilderment
cheerful	happy	cheer up
concerned	somewhat worried	concern, concerns
confusing	puzzling, hard to understand	confused, confusion
critical	evaluating or judging	critic, critically
cynical	untrusting	cynic, cynically
defensive	protective of oneself	defensively
determined	set on a particular course of action	determination

Mood and Tone Words (continued)

Mood or Tone Word	Definition	Similar Words
disappointing	less than expected	disappointed, disappointment
discouraging	not hopeful	discouraged, discouragement
encouraging	hopeful, uplifting	encouraged, encouragement
energetic	very active	energy, energetically
entertainment	something fun	entertained, entertaining
enthusiastic	excited	enthusiasm, enthusiastically
exciting	energizing	excited, excitement, excitedly
frustrating	difficult and irritating	frustrated, frustration
fun	amusing, exhilarating	
funny	humorous	
happy	glad or content	happiness, happily
honest	truthful	honesty, honestly
hopeful	expectant	hope, hopefulness, hopefully
humorous	funny	humor, humorously
hysterical	emotionally out of control	hysteria, hysterically
idealistic	reflecting or desiring perfection	idealism, idealistically
indifferent	without strong feelings one way or another	indifferently
ironic	similar in some ways but different in a surprising or strange way	irony, ironically
judgmental	evaluative, critical	judgment, judged
mad	angry, *or sometimes* crazy	madly
matter-of-fact	without a show of emotion	matter-of-factly
meditative	quiet and reflective	meditation
melancholy	sad	melancholic
negative	critical or discouraged	negatively

Mood and Tone Words (continued)

Mood or Tone Word	Definition	Similar Words
nervous	jumpy, expectantly worried, on edge	nervously, nervousness, nerves
neutral	fair, unbiased, impartial	neutrality
nostalgic	sentimental about a previous time or place	nostalgia
optimistic	expectant and hopeful	optimism
persuasive	convincing	persuasion
pessimistic	not hopeful	pessimism
questioning	wondering, investigating, challenging	questioned
realistic	without false hopes or expectations	realistically
reflective	meditative, contemplative	reflection
regretful	sorrowful	regret, regrets
relaxed	calm, not tense	relaxing
sad	unhappy	sadly, sadness
sarcastic	cutting or critical, and ironic	sarcasm, sarcastically
satirical	witty and sarcastic	satire
serious	thoughtful or purposeful	seriousness, seriously
sincere	honest	sincerity, sincerely
skeptical	doubting	skepticism
solitude	aloneness	solitary
straightforward	direct, unconcealed	straightforwardly
surprising	unexpected	surprise, surprised
thoughtful	considerate, or reflective	thoughtfulness
truthful	honest	truth
unconcerned	not worried	unconcern
unhappy	sad, miserable	unhappiness
unrealistic	with false hopes or expectations	unrealistically
wishful	desirous	wish, wishfully
wonder	awe	wonderment
worried	anxious, very concerned	worry, worrying

(For a more extensive list of words that show tone and mood along with their Spanish translations, see <u>Miss Runner's ELD Home Page</u> on the Web at http://www.elite.net/~runner/eld/tone.html. The same list of words with Hmong translations is at http://www.elite.net/~runner/eld/toneeh.html. Both pages are by Jennifer Runner, English Language Development Department, Atwater High School, Atwater, California.)

Note: The following example questions do not refer to a particular story. They are just samples of the kind of questions about **mood** *and* **tone** *that you may find on the CAHSEE.*

Example Question About Mood:

Example Question 1:

Which of the following phrases describes the mood of this story (or *poem*, or *reading*, etc.)?

A   envy and desire

B   suspicion and anger

C   surprise and pleasure

D   wonder and shame

Example Questions about Tone:

- Which word best describes the tone of this poem?

- What tone does the writer portray in the story?

The answers can be any of the words from the Mood and Tone Words list (see pages 46–48), or any other description of the *feel* of the reading selection.

Example Question 2:

Which of the following pairs of words from the reading establishes a tone of humor and hopefulness?

A   reflecting thoughtfully

B   laughing expectantly

C   wishing quietly

D   reacting angrily

B is the best answer.

Analyzing Plot, Conflict, and Resolution

The *plot* of a novel or short story tells what happens in the story, and how one event can lead to other events. Stories include a *main character* (sometimes referred to as the *protagonist* or the *hero*) and a standard plot contains at least one problem, or *conflict*, that the main character must face.

Conflict is important because it makes a story interesting. Readers want to learn how the story ends, and if the main character is successful or not. The way the conflict turns out is called the *resolution*, and it can be either a successful resolution (a happy ending), an unsuccessful resolution (an unhappy ending), or a combination of the two.

The term *internal conflict* is used to describe a character who is struggling with more than one urge or impulse.

You will probably not see any questions that ask you to describe the plot or to identify the main character, the conflict, or the resolution on the CAHSEE. However, these terms may be used in other questions that ask you to analyze the characters in a story. For more information about analyzing characters, see the following section: "Analyzing a Character's Personality, Feelings, and Relationships."

Analyzing a Character's Personality, Feelings, and Relationships

Definition of Character

Characters are the people in stories and other literature. They are a very important way for the author to communicate the *meaning* of the story, even though most stories and poems can be interpreted in more than one way. When a character is the one telling the story, sometimes that character may be referred to as the *narrator*.

Simple or Complex

In literature, each character shows the readers something about human nature. Sometimes a character shows us only a very *narrow* or specific part of human nature, such as the evil enemies of Superman and Batman, or an overprotective father, or the boy who cried "wolf" when there wasn't one. Also, characters can remain the same throughout the story, or they may change.

The word *trait* is used to describe a character's nature. For example, one character might show the trait of being sneaky, while another one might show the trait of blaming someone else.

Other times, characters can be very *complex*, with a battle for good and evil going on inside of them, a tug-of-war between the desire to trust someone and the desire to protect themselves, or another complicated conflict.

Environment, Background, and Motivation

A character's *environment* (the situation she or he is in) or *background* (previous experiences) can affect his or her reactions, *motivations*, and goals. *Motivation* is the reason that characters act or think as they do.

Relationships and Interactions Between Characters

One very important way to analyze a character is to understand the *relationships* between that character and the other characters in the story, and how the characters interact with each other.

Tips for Answering Questions about Character

The following tips will help you to answer the questions about characters on the CAHSEE.

- First, pay attention to what the characters say and how they say it. If the story tells what the character is thinking, pay attention to that too.

- Next, pay attention to the actions that the characters do, because actions often provide a great deal of information about a character.

- Finally, pay attention to what the other characters and/or the narrator say or think about the character that you are analyzing.

Note: The following example questions do not refer to a particular story. They are just samples of the kind of questions about **characters** *that you may find on the CAHSEE.*

Example Question 1:

How is Martin's personality in the story?

A   supportive and understanding

B   funny and enthusiastic

C   depressed and unhappy

D   angry and antisocial

Example Question 2:

Which phrase from the story best describes the tender part of Max's personality?

Example Question 3:

Why does the narrator spend so much time alone?

Example Question 4:

Which statement from the passage best demonstrates Juana's motivation for enrolling in summer school?

Example Question 5:

Which of the following best shows the relationship between Clint and his family?

Example Question 6:

How do Joe's friends and family react to his new hobby?

A   His friends are happy but his family is worried.

B   His friends are jealous but his family is proud.

C   His friends are unhappy but his family is impressed.

D   His friends are amused but his family is annoyed.

Identifying Literary Devices (Techniques and Strategies)

Good writers use a variety of techniques and strategies, also called *literary devices*, which are carefully chosen to accomplish their purposes for writing each selection. On the CAHSEE you may see questions that include the following literary terms:

- Setting

- Imagery

- Symbolism

- Allegory

- Dialogue, Soliloquy, and Asides

- Fact and Opinion

- Statistics

- Repetition

(The literary devices *Metaphor* and *Simile* are covered in the section on *Figurative Language*, in Chapter 1.)

*Note: Many of the following questions do not refer to a particular story. They are just samples of the kind of questions about **literary devices** that you may find on the CAHSEE.*

Setting

The *setting* is the location and time that a play or other piece of literature takes place. The *setting* tells the reader what the place looks like, what year and season it is, what time of day it is, or other important background details. Some reading selections include very detailed settings, while others provide only a few details about the setting.

Example Question:

Which of the following sentences best describes the setting of the story (play, poem)?

A Immediately after the movie ended, the police chased three suspects through the theater.

B The "movie theater" consisted of just a screen and a few rows of benches, with no walls, situated right on the sandy beach.

C The movie was shown in English with Spanish subtitles.

D The movie was a comedy about a French detective who was conducting a major investigation.

Setting shows the location and background information about where the story took place. C and D show background information, but the best answer is B because it also includes the place.

Imagery

Imagery is when a writer uses the senses to give readers a mental picture, to help them experience literature as if it were *real*. Imagery can include any of the five senses: sight, hearing, touch/feeling, taste, or smell, and may include a *metaphor*, a *simile*, or *personification*.

For example, in order to help readers relate to a story about a summer picnic, the writer might describe the taste of corn on the cob that has been slathered with butter, wrapped in foil, and grilled. By appealing to the senses, the writer brings readers into the setting and the action of the story.

Many times, imagery has a *figurative* meaning rather than an actual meaning. For example, an author might write, "Owning a car gave me my first taste of freedom." This might sound strange because *freedom* is not something that really has a physical taste. The sense of taste is an *image*, used here in order to help the reader understand better the full experience of freedom, a freedom as real and delicious as a tasty meal.

Example Question:

Which of the following lines from the reading contains an example of imagery?

A No one received an "A" on the first quiz, but after we studied hard for the next two weeks, we did much better on the second one.

B   We ran to the park to play for a half hour before we had to start our homework.

C   The students arrived in a large group, excited about the upcoming basketball game.

D   The teacher's words of praise for my project made me feel warm all day.

The best answer is D. The warm feeling is an example of *imagery*—in this case, a physical feeling—which helps the reader experience the events of the story and makes them seem and feel *real.*

Symbolism

Symbolism is the use of real things to represent abstract ideas. For example, a story about a young man's encounter with a snake might symbolize the necessity of facing our fears in order to defeat them. A single flower in the middle of a concrete city might symbolize hope, and the ocean might represent the unknown.

Example Question:

What do the Sequoia redwood trees symbolize in the following lines from the story?

When we arrived at Sequoia National Park, I was amazed at the size of the redwood trees. Some of them were so big that people could drive a car through the middle of the trunk. To me, they were more than just trees. They were promises that my life, too, would have stature and meaning.

A   hope for the future

B   power and beauty

C   conservation work

D   the need to work hard

The word *promises* indicates the future, and hope. Answer A is the best choice.

Allegory

An allegory is a story that represents something different from what it says on the surface. One famous allegory is J. R. R. Tolkien's series of books *The Lord of the Rings*. These adventure stories show us a parallel world where little people called *hobbits* travel with elves and dwarfs as they struggle against evil within themselves and against enemies in a race to save their world.

Dialogue, Soliloquy, and Asides

Dialogue is the conversation between two or more characters. A *soliloquy* is a speech that contains the thoughts and reflections of one character alone, and is often rather long. *Asides* are messages directed to the audience and not heard by the other characters in the play.

In Shakespeare's *Hamlet*, for example, there is an example of an extended soliloquy that begins as follows:

To be, or not to be, that is the question:
Whether 'tis nobler in the mind to suffer
The slings and arrows of outrageous fortune;
Or to take arms against a sea of troubles,
And by opposing, end them: to die, to sleep
No more....*

---

*As found online at The Monologue Shop,
http://www.themonologueshop.com/samples.php?s_sceneID=751.

Example Question:

Which of the following literary devices is found in this selection from the reading (story, poem)?

"My son, I forbid you to marry so far beneath your station. You stand to inherit the dual throne of Austria and Hungary, and she is but the daughter of a lowly baronet." As the empress swept out of the room, she barely heard the prince's soft reply: "But mother, she is worth more to me than all the empires of history."

A   allegory

B   soliloquy

C   dialogue

D   symbolism

The selection contains a conversation between the prince and his mother, the empress. The best answer is C, dialogue.

Fact and Opinion

Facts include those points of information that can be verified, which do not change based on whether people believe them or not. *Opinions* represent judgments, evaluations, feelings, emotions, or personal reactions, and are different for different people.

For example, the statement "The Declaration of Independence was signed in 1776," is a *fact* because it can be checked in an encyclopedia or other reference book. On the other hand, the statement "The Declaration of Independence is one of the greatest documents of all time" is an *opinion* because it evaluates, or judges, the importance of this document. Even though this statement represents the opinions of many credible sources, it is still an opinion and not a fact.

Example Question:

Which of the following strategies is not used (in a particular reading, article, or selection)?

A   repetition

B   expert opinion

C   scientific fact

D   dialogue

If you are familiar with all of these terms, you should be able to check the reading to see which ones are used, and eliminate all but one of the answers.

Statistics

Statistics are *numbers* that provide evidence, one of several ways of providing effective support for the points that a writer makes. For example, the statement "California has more than 34 million residents" includes a statistic. Another statistic appears in the sentence "San Francisco had a total of 12.3 inches of rain in April."

Statistics may be *true*, *false*, or *exaggerated*. The careful use of statistics can improve the effectiveness of many types of writing, including persuasive essays and business letters.

Questions about statistics will probably ask whether statistics are used in the reading. Some questions may ask why statistics are used in a particular story. In both cases, look for an answer that shows *what point* is supported by the use of statistics.

Example Question:

> **What point is supported by the use of statistics in the following essay?**

Repetition

Repetition is the use of the same ideas, images, or plot elements (things that happen in the story) more than once in the same story. By using repetition, writers emphasize a point, create an effect, or call the reader's attention to a certain part of the story.

Example Question:

What is the purpose of the repetition of the words *wet* and *water* in the following selection?

From behind the thick Plexiglas™ barrier we could see the huge mammal gathering speed as it swam through the water. At that moment we suddenly noticed that the wet area extended beyond the walkway where we were standing, several rows up into the audience. The concrete floor under the wet plastic seats was covered with a film of water from previous splashes, and we were the only adults foolish or ignorant enough to have placed ourselves in the middle of "the splash zone."

As the killer whale leaped high out of the water directly in front of us, we woke up to the fact that water would soon play a very prominent part in our day at Sea World.

A   To remind the reader that killer whales live in the water

B   To help organize the order in which things happen in the story

C   To emphasize the importance of water in their day at Sea World

D   To indicate that the writer was unhappy about getting splashed

The best answer is C. Repetition gives emphasis to the words that are repeated, in this case, *wet* and *water*.

Another type of question on some CAHSEE exams asks <u>why</u> the author uses repetition in a story. The reason might be to emphasize the ideas that are repeated, or to make a point that is important to the story.

Identifying Types of Literature (Genres)

The CAHSEE may ask you to identify the type, or *genre*, of a selection of literature. The four main categories of literature that you will see on the CAHSEE are *plays*, *poetry*, *fiction,* and *nonfiction.*

Please note that the CAHSEE does not include specific questions about particular writings or authors, for example, *Macbeth* or *Shakespeare*.

Plays

Dramatic literature includes various types of *plays*, poems, and certain short stories. A *play* is a story that has been written to be performed on the stage as live theater, with real people. Type of plays include *comedies*, *tragedies*, *dramas*, and *dramatic monologues*.

Comedy

A *comedy* is dramatic writing that uses humor to make its point. Plays that include humorous incidents, ironic comments, jokes, plays on words, back-and-forth put-downs, or funny remarks by the characters are examples of comedy. The main purpose of a comedy is to entertain the audience.

Tragedy

A *tragedy* is a play that has sad events and usually a sad ending. These are usually easy to recognize.

Drama

While any play can technically be considered a *drama*, this term usually refers to a play that deals with a serious topic.

Dramatic Monologue

A *dramatic monologue* is dramatic writing in which only one person speaks.

Poetry

Poetry is spoken or written literature that uses specific words, sounds, rhythms, and mental associations to create certain feelings, moods, or emotions in the reader or listener. Poems may or may not rhyme, and there are many types of poems. Three poetic structures that you may be asked to identify on the CAHSEE include *ballads*, *sonnets*, and *couplets*.

Ballad

A *ballad* is a song or poem that tells a story and includes repetition of part of the lines of poetry, but with some variation the second time. The stories told in ballads are often folk tales about love, knights, or supernatural events of long ago.

Ballads, as well as many other poems, are sometimes divided into *stanzas*, which are groups of a certain number of lines, similar to paragraphs in other types of writing.

Couplet

A *couplet* consists of two rhyming lines of poetry in a row. Shakespeare's sonnets end in a couplet, like the following from *Romeo and Juliet*:

Good night! Good night! Parting is such sweet sorrow
That I shall say good-night till it be morrow.

Sonnet

A *sonnet* is a type of poem with a very specific structure that always includes 14 lines. There are two types of sonnets, the *Italian* (also called *petrarchan*) and the *English* (also called *Shakespearean*), each with a different rhyming pattern.

Here is an example of a sonnet by William Shakespeare:

Sonnet 116

Let me not to the marriage of true minds
Admit impediments. Love is not love
Which alters when it alteration finds,
Or bends with the remover to remove.
O no, it is an ever fixèd mark

That looks on tempests and is never shaken;
It is the star to every wand'ring barque,
Whose worth's unknown, although his height be taken.
Love's not time's fool, though rosy lips and cheeks
Within his bending sickle's compass come.
Love alters not with his brief hours and weeks,
But bears it out even to the edge of doom.
If this be error and upon me proved,
I never writ, nor no man ever loved.

(To hear audio readings of Shakespeare's sonnets, visit
http://town.hall.org/Archives/radio/IMS/HarperAudio/
020994_harp_ITH.html).

Fiction

Fiction includes *short stories, novels,* and *novellas*.

Short Story

A *short story* is a type of fiction that provides insight into the characters and the action in a very short space. As a result, there are usually not many characters, and the action is usually limited to one main story line.

Novel

A *novel* is a longer type of fiction that has the length necessary to develop the action of the story over the course of many events. As a result, readers are able to understand the characters in a novel more fully than those in a short story. The main purpose of some novels—such as romances, westerns, or science fiction—is often to entertain the reader. The other main purpose of many novels is to show aspects of human nature and society—the bad as well as the good.

Novella

A *novella* is a fictional story that falls somewhere between a long short story and a short novel in length.

Nonfiction

Types of *nonfiction* that you might see on the CAHSEE include *articles, essays, biographies*, and *autobiographies*.

Article

An *article* is a separate piece of writing that is included in a longer publication such as a newspaper or magazine. The main purpose of most articles is to *inform* the reader.

Essay

In an *essay*, the writer presents an idea to the reader. Essays are often personal, and may include personal experiences to back up the point that the author wishes to make. Some essays are designed to persuade the reader of an idea, while others just speculate about an idea. (See Chapters 8-10 for more detailed information about essays).

Biography and Autobiography

A *biography* is a story about someone's life, while an *autobiography* is a biography about the writer's own life.

Example Question 1:

> **This selection is an example of which of the following genres of writing?**

The answers to this question can be any of the types of writing listed above. Some questions may have very general answers (a poem, a short story, an article, a biography), but sometimes the answers are more specific (a persuasive essay, a biographical essay, a third-person short story, an informational article).

The section on *Analyzing the Purpose of a Reading* earlier in this chapter may also help you choose the correct answer to this type of question.

Example Question 2:

> **How does the reader know that this selection is a sonnet?**

> **A**   It has a sad ending.

> **B**   It tells a story of love and romance.

> **C**   Its purpose is to inform the reader.

> **D**   It is a poem with 14 lines.

The definition of a sonnet is that it is a poem with 14 lines, so D is the best answer. Even though answers A and B may also contain correct information, they are also true of many other types of writing. Similar questions may ask about *tragedies, comedies, ballads,* or *dramatic monologues.*

Analyzing and Evaluating Supporting Information

Support

Whether the purpose of an essay, article, or research paper is to entertain, persuade, or inform, the basic organization of the ideas is similar. There is a *main idea* (also called a *thesis* or *controlling idea*) and *supporting information*. The *support* for the main idea can include facts, examples, details, statistics, expert opinion, or supporting ideas that can themselves be supported, as shown below.

- Main Idea (Thesis) supported by:

  — *Examples*, *details*, *statistics*, *facts*, and/or *quotes* that support the main idea.

  — *Ideas* that support the main idea (called *supporting ideas*, *main points*, or *key points*) supported by:

    - - - *Examples*, *details*, *statistics*, *facts* and/or *quotes* that support the supporting ideas

Support for the Main Idea

Some CAHSEE questions ask about sentences that support the *main idea* of a reading. The best way to answer these questions is to discover what the main idea of the reading is, and then determine which of the sentences provides information that helps make that point—or sometimes, which of the sentences <u>does not</u> help to make the point.

The example questions about *support* are based on the following reading. However, on the actual CAHSEE, there will probably be only one question about *support* in any particular reading.

(The following reading is from the online article "Parchment and Paper" in the *Paper, Leather, Clay & Stone Exhibition* of the Division of Rare and Manuscript Collections, Cornell University Library, and can be accessed at <u>http://rmc.library.cornell.edu/Paper-exhibit/paper3.html</u>. Used by permission.)

Parchment and Paper

Parchment first emerged as a common writing surface in response to a shortage of papyrus in Pergamon in the second century BCE. It was made of goatskin that had been soaked in lime and scraped to remove hair. The surface was then burnished with pumice to create a smooth surface for writing. Even finer than parchment, vellum was made of calfskin and often coated to make the surface exceptionally smooth.

Paper, like papyrus, is made from plants—usually flax or cotton. The fibers are soaked until they soften and separate; the resulting paste is then spread and formed on a screen, pressed, and polished. Developed in China, the technique of papermaking spread east via migrating Mongolians and ultimately to the Maya in Mexico, and west via Samarkand to Islamic lands and finally Europe.

The smooth surface of parchment allowed for a finer, more controlled hand, and the reed brush used for papyrus was replaced with a firmer goose quill pen. Paper was even more accepting; writing could be accomplished generally with an animal-hair brush, ink pen, lead pencil, or even a lump of charcoal. The introduction of parchment and paper had a dramatic effect on the appearance and quantity of text that could be produced conveniently. Both materials were conducive to use in a codex, or book-like, format, and both could accommodate illustration and decoration as easily as they did writing. They would transform the way many cultures viewed the role and function of text.

The art of fine writing was prized in East Asia where the ideographic alphabet limited literacy to an elite few. In China and Japan, brushwork and image took on the same aesthetic. In the Islamic world, where the word was more highly valued than the image, calligraphy played a special role in the making of the Qur'an. And before the advent of printing in medieval Europe, scribes copied religious and secular documents, often embellishing them with illustrations and fanciful letters. In all of these societies, the scribe and calligrapher enjoyed high status.

Example Question 1:

Adding which of the following sentences would best support the main idea of the article?

A   Parchment is still used in many countries in the world today.

B   A unique writing style was developed in Burma.

C   Illustrated medieval manuscripts were usually referred to as "illuminated" manuscripts.

D   Parchment and paper were easier to use than papyrus.

The main idea of the article is that paper and parchment had a dramatic effect on the amount and quality of writing that could be produced. Of the choices listed, only D supports this idea.

Example Question 2:

Which of the following lines from the article best supports the main idea?

A   Parchment first emerged as a common writing surface in response to a shortage of papyrus in Pergamon in the second century BCE.

B   Paper, like papyrus, is made from plants—usually flax or cotton.

C   Paper was even more accepting; writing could be accomplished generally with an animal-hair brush, ink pen, lead pencil, or even a lump of charcoal.

D   In all of these societies, the scribe and calligrapher enjoyed high status.

The best answer is C because it states that paper made writing easier, which supports the main idea that paper and parchment had a great effect on the amount and quality of writing that could be produced.

Support for Key Points

In addition to questions about support for the *main idea*, some questions on the CAHSEE ask about support for a *supporting idea* (or *key point*) in the essay. Read each question carefully to determine whether it is asking about the *main idea* of the reading or about a *key point*.

Example Question 1:

Which information in the article supports the idea that writing became a fine art in Asia?

A   In medieval Europe, scribes decorated documents with illustrations and fanciful letters.

B   In China and Japan, brushwork and image took on the same aesthetic.

C   Parchment and paper could easily be used in book form.

D   In the Islamic world…calligraphy played a special role in the making of the Qur'an.

A refers to Europe, D refers mainly to the Middle East, and C is generally true. Only B refers to fine art in *Asia*.

Example Question 2:

Which of the following ideas is supported by details or evidence in the article?

A   Scribes and calligraphers were held in high esteem in many societies.

B   Vellum was more common than parchment.

C   Everyone needs to learn to write well.

D   Papyrus is still used for printing books in many countries in the world today.

The statement "Scribes and calligraphers were held in high esteem in many societies" is supported by information about Asia, the Islamic world, and Europe. The information in B, C, and D is not contained in the article, so A is the best answer.

Evaluating Paragraph Unity

In each body paragraph, all of the information must support the key point or main idea of that paragraph in one way or another. When all of the sentences work together to support the main idea of the paragraph, we say that the paragraph has *unity*.

One of the types of questions that may appear on the CAHSEE is to ask which sentence does NOT belong in its paragraph. Always look for the sentence that is on a different topic or that does not support the key point of the paragraph.

Example Question:

Which of the following sentences does NOT belong in this paragraph?

Many universities are now offering early admission to students who make an early commitment to a particular university. Students that are accepted early benefit because they no longer have to worry about being admitted. The universities benefit because they can spread out the admission process over a longer time instead of crunching all of the applicants into the same short time period. Some students apply to many colleges.

A   Many universities are now offering early admission to students who make an early commitment to a particular university.

B   Students that are accepted early benefit because they no longer have to worry about being admitted.

C   The universities benefit because they can spread out the admission process over a longer time instead of crunching all of the applicants into the same short time period.

D   Some students apply to many colleges.

The best answer is "D" because it does not support the key point of this paragraph, the possibility of early admission to universities.

For more information on *Finding the Main Idea*, see Chapter 2.

CAHSEE
English-Language Arts

Section 3:

Writing Skills

Writing
Strategies

Writing strategies that appear in the Analysis of Writing Strategies section of the CAHSEE multiple-choice questions include the following:

- Using Specific Details and Language

- Using the Active Voice

- Sentence Combining

This chapter also includes two additional writing strategies that are helpful for some of the questions in other sections:

- Paraphrasing

- Summarizing

In addition, all of the writing strategies that are reviewed in this chapter can be helpful for writing the essay on the CAHSEE exam.

Using Specific Details and Language

One important strategy for writers is to use *specific details.* Specific details make the written words seem more real and interesting to the readers. For example, when describing a trip to the local mountains, it would not be very interesting just to say, "We saw a lot of trees." It would be better to include specific details that indicate what kind of trees they were, how many you saw (hundreds? dozens?), how big they were, what shades of green, brown, or other colors they were, something about the shape of the needles or leaves or of the trees themselves, and any details that might help readers see the picture in their mind's eye and feel as if they are really there.

When you write, you are already familiar with the people and objects that you describe in your writing, but your readers do not have that advantage. Readers will have a better idea of what you want to say if you use very specific language. Avoid words like *big*, *good*, *bad*, *warm*, *pretty*, *fine*, *nice*, and any language that is vague. Instead, use expressions like "as big as our house," "better than hot chocolate on a cold morning," "so hot I couldn't touch the pan," "a crimson and tangerine sunset."

Example Questions:

The following is the rough draft of a short story about one person's experience with an unfamiliar type of food. It contains some language that should be more specific. Read the story and answer the questions that follow.

Guacamole

My father-in-law Roy Roberts was born in Oklahoma and raised in West Texas, but when he got to California he tried a well-known Japanese <u>thing</u> (1) called *sushi*, which consisted of seaweed and rice wrapped around cooked or raw fish and cut into bite-sized slices. When the tray of sushi arrived on the day this story took place, Roy looked it over and picked out one of the round slices to try.

Next to the sushi was <u>some</u> (2) smooth green guacamole in a tiny paper cup about the size of a big thimble. Guacamole is a delicious mash of avocados with spices or Mexican salsa. Sometimes it has sour cream mixed in to give it a lighter green color and richer taste.

Roy put the entire tablespoon of creamy guacamole on his piece of sushi and started to chew vigorously, until one second later when a signal started in his mouth and quickly spread to his throat and nose on the way to his brain.

That signal said, "HELP!"

That's when Roy learned that the little dab of green stuff wasn't really guacamole. It was a very strong Japanese horseradish paste, green like guacamole, called *wasabi*. The way people are supposed to eat it is to get a tiny bit of it on the tip of a chopstick, mix it well into a puddle of soy sauce on the plate, and dip the sushi into the sauce.

After Roy recovered from that episode, he was always quick to recommend that "guacamole" to his buddies, but he never took another bite of it himself.

Example Question 1:

Which sentence from the story explains specifically what the green paste was?

A   Next to the sushi was about a tablespoon of smooth green guacamole in a tiny paper cup about the size of a big thimble.

B   Guacamole is a delicious mash of avocados with spices or Mexican salsa.

C   Sometimes it has sour cream mixed in to give it a lighter green color and richer taste.

D   It was a very strong Japanese horseradish paste, green like guacamole, called *wasabi*.

Answer A describes the amount and color of the wasabi, B explains what guacamole is, and C gives more information about guacamole. Answer D is the best because it is the only one that explains specifically what the green paste was.

Example Question 2:

To make the meaning more specific, which of the following answers should the underlined word labeled (2) be changed to?

A   a little

B   about a tablespoon of

C a small amount of

D a quantity of

Of these answers, B is the most specific. The other three answers are very general.

Example Question 3:

Which of the following words is the most specific way to express the meaning of the word *thing*, labeled (1) in the story?

A stuff

B item

C food

D import

Food is the most specific answer, so C is the best answer.

Using the Active Voice

Active voice is a grammar term that means that the subject of the sentence is active—that is, the subject performs the action of the verb. *Passive voice* means that the subject of the sentence is passive, and receives the effect of the action. (See Chapters 5 and 6 for more information about subjects and verbs.)

Some questions on the CAHSEE will ask you to choose a better way to express a sentence that is written in the *passive voice*. While there are some very important uses of the *passive voice*, sentences are often more powerful and more interesting when they are written in the *active voice*.

To determine whether a sentence is in the *active voice* or the *passive voice*, look for a form of the verb *to be—be, am, are, is, was, were, been,* or *being*—that is used as a helping verb together with the *past participle* of a main verb. Past participles of regular verbs end in *-ed*, but you must memorize the past participles of irregular verbs, such as *broken, brought, eaten, gone, had,* and *taken*.

Examples of Active Voice and Passive Voice Sentences:

Example Sentence 1—Active Voice:

        S   V
My friend <u>bought</u> this shirt at the mall.

In Sentence 1, the subject is "My friend," the one who performed the action of buying the shirt. When the subject performs the action, the sentence is in the active voice.

Example Sentence 2—Passive Voice:

        S   V
This shirt <u>was bought</u> at the mall.

In Sentence 2, the subject is "This shirt." The shirt did not perform an action; instead, it was acted upon. When the subject is acted upon instead of performing an action, we say that the sentence is in the *passive voice*.

Directions:

Choose the best answer to replace the underlined words in Example Questions 1 and 2. If the original wording is the best, choose "(Leave as is.)"

Example Question 1.

> **At the last basketball game of the season, <u>awards were received by many players</u>.**
>
> **A** ... many players received awards.
>
> **B** ... many players were given awards.
>
> **C** ... awards were given to many players.
>
> **D** (Leave as is.)

Of the four answers, only answer A is active voice, and it is the best answer. The other three are passive because they have the helping verb *were*, plus the past participle of the main verb, and the subject receives the action, instead of performing the action.

Example Question 2.

One tradition in our family is that <u>Thanksgiving dinner is prepared by all of us working together</u>.

A   ... all of us working together are preparing Thanksgiving dinner.

B   ... we all work together to prepare Thanksgiving dinner.

C   ... by all of us working together, Thanksgiving dinner is prepared.

D   (Leave as is.)

The best answer is B because it is active voice and it is clearly written. A is also active voice, but it is somewhat clumsy, and C and D are both passive voice.

Sentence Combining

Sentence combining is a writing strategy that can help you write better sentences. It consists of making larger, more advanced sentences by joining smaller sentences together with sentence connectors, using effective connecting words and correct punctuation. (See Chapter 5 for more information about specific sentence patterns.) Also, repeated subjects, verbs and other words are often eliminated.

The four points to remember about sentence combining are the following:

1)   The sentence must sound natural.

2)   Sentence connectors must have the correct meaning.

3)   The correct punctuation must be used for each type of sentence connector that you are using.

4)   Repeated words should be eliminated.

Example of Sentence Combining:

Original Sentences: Catalina Island is a beautiful place. Visitors can hike, camp, or go kayaking in sea caves. They can also sail on a glass-bottom boat. They might even take a jeep ride to see buffalo and other wild animals.

There are several ways to combine these sentences into one longer and more effective sentence. Here is one of them:

Catalina Island is a beautiful place where visitors can hike, camp, go kayaking in sea caves, sail on a glass-bottom boat, or maybe even take a jeep ride to see buffalo and other wild animals.

You can practice your sentence skills by combining sentences in the papers you write for school assignments and correcting any sentence structure mistakes that the teacher marks.

The CAHSEE may include a question about sentence combining as a writing strategy. It is important to remember that many writers use sentence combining in order to make their writing more effective.

Example Question:

What is the best way to combine the following sentences?

By studying hard, Sharon was able to raise her score a lot. She passed the test.

A   Sharon was able to raise her score by studying hard a lot, so she passed the test.

B   By studying hard. Sharon was able to raise her score a lot, which she passed the test.

C   Sharon was able to raise her score a lot, which she passed the test by studying hard.

D   By studying hard, Sharon was able to raise her score a lot, so she passed the test.

D is the only answer that sounds natural and follows a correct sentence pattern, so it is the best choice.

For more information about sentence connectors, see Chapter 5.

Paraphrasing and Summarizing

When writing the essay on the CAHSEE, *paraphrasing*, *quoting*, and *summarizing* can be important tools. This section covers paraphrasing and summarizing. For more information on quotations, see Chapter 7. If you are asked to write a Response to a Literature Essay or an Analytical Essay, any of these three strategies can be used to support your points by referring back to information in the reading. (For more information about writing an essay that asks you to respond to a reading, see Chapter 10.)

Paraphrasing

Paraphrasing means *using your own words to report what someone has said or written*. The Reading Comprehension section of the CAHSEE may include some questions that ask which is the best way to reword a badly written sentence or to show that you understand information in a reading selection.

The most important thing to remember about paraphrased material is that it must include *all* of the information from the original reading, in different words.

Summarizing

Summarizing means using your own words to report *just the main points* of what someone has said or written. It is a useful tool for beginning one of the essays mentioned above. By summarizing the main point of the reading, you show that you understand it. Also, you may see a question like the following in the Reading Comprehension questions:

Example Question:

Which sentence from the document BEST summarizes the author's main point?

(For more information about *Finding the Main Idea*, see Chapter 2.)

Recognizing and Writing Correct Sentences

The Writing Conventions section of the CAHSEE may ask several multiple-choice questions about sentences and sentence connectors. Knowing how to write a variety of correct sentences can also help you get a high score on the essay portions of the test. This chapter includes the following topics:

- Identifying Subjects and Verbs

- Definitions of Clause, Phrase, and Sentence

- Types of Sentences

- Avoiding Common Sentence Errors: Fragments, Run-on Sentences, and Comma Splices

- Summary of Sentence Punctuation

- More About Sentences: Phrases, Placement of Modifiers, and Parallel Structure.

Identifying Subjects and Verbs

The ability to identify *subjects* and *verbs* will help you know where to end a sentence or use a connector to join it to another sentence.

Subject

In everyday language, the *subject* that someone studies or writes about means the same as the *topic*. However, the word *subject* has a completely different meaning when used to explain grammar and sentence structure.

In most sentences, the *subject* is the person or thing that performs the action in a sentence.

Verb

The *verb* is the word that shows the action of a sentence. In addition to *action verbs*, some verbs are *helping verbs* (also called *auxiliary verbs*) and others are *linking verbs*, which connect or link the subject to the rest of the sentence.

The subjects and verbs in the following example sentences are marked with S and V. Also, the subjects are underlined and the verbs are in bold print. Notice that both subjects and verbs sometimes include more than one word.

Examples of subjects and verbs:

          S   V

1.   <u>Rachel</u> **wore** a black dress and pearls for the formal dance.

          S   V

2.   <u>The van</u> **needs** to have its brakes checked.

            S   V

3.   <u>Marsha and Russ</u> **have put** in a new cement walkway to their front door.

                   S   V

4.   <u>Setting aside a time to study each day</u> **will help** you do well in school.

                      S   V

5.   <u>The communications program at the nearby college</u> **is** an excellent one.

Definitions of Clause, Phrase, and Sentence

Clause

A *clause* is a group of words that contains a subject and a verb.

Phrase

A *phrase* is a group of words that does <u>not</u> contain a complete subject and verb. Phrases are often useful for adding descriptive details and other information.

Sentence

A *sentence* consists of *at least* one clause. Sentences that have more than one clause need to be connected by one of the various types of sentence connectors, using correct punctuation. Each type of connector must be punctuated differently, as seen in the following section.

Types of Sentences

This section of the chapter includes *simple sentences*, *basic compound sentences*, *basic complex sentences*, *advanced compound sentences*, and *complex sentences with relative clauses*.

Simple Sentences

A *simple sentence* is a sentence that includes just one clause (one subject and verb, or SV). It may also include one or more phrases. The following sentences are all simple sentences:

Example 1.

        S   V
The <u>bell</u> rang.

Example 2.

        S   V
The <u>bell</u> rang, signaling the end of class.

Example 3.

                          S
A short time later, the <u>bell</u> in the main administration

                  V
building started ringing.

Basic Compound Sentences

A *basic compound sentence* has at least two subject and verb combinations connected by a *coordinating conjunction*. These include the words *for* (meaning because), *and*, *nor*, *but*, *or*, *yet* and *so*. An easy way to memorize this list is to make a word out of the first letters: f a n b o y s. In this book they will be referred to as "Group A Connectors." With two exceptions, whenever these words are used to connect two clauses (SVs), they must follow this pattern:

SV , Group A Connector SV.

Exceptions:

1) Short sentences do not need a comma with Group A connectors.

2) The Group A word *nor* follows slightly different rules.

The words *for* and *yet* have more than one meaning, but when they are used as sentence connectors, *for* means *because*, and *yet* means *but*.

The following sentences are all examples of basic compound sentences.

Example 1.

Patris felt relaxed, for she had just returned from a restful vacation.

Example 2.

>   We finished the test early, but it was not easy.

Example 3.

>   Students can study at home, or they can study in the library.

Example 4.

>   The bell rang and the students left. (Because this sentence is so short, no comma is needed—see Exception 1 above.)

Example 5.

>   Tomatoes are not expensive to grow, nor do they require much care.

>   *Note:* The Group A connector *nor* requires a slightly different word order. With *nor*, the pattern is S V , Group A **V S**. (If you are not comfortable using *nor* as a sentence connector, you probably should not try to use it on the CAHSEE essay.)

Basic Complex Sentences

>   A *basic complex sentence* has at least two clauses (SVs) connected by a <u>subordinating</u> *conjunction*. In this book, we will refer to them as "Group B Connectors." There are more than 30 of these connectors, including the words listed below. Some Group B connectors consist of more than one word.

Subordinating Conjunctions (Group B Connectors)

after	although	as
as if	as soon as	as though
because	even though	how
however	if	since
so (so that)	than	that
though	unless	what
whatever	when	whenever
where	whereas	whether

With very few exceptions, whenever these words are used to connect two clauses (SVs), they must follow one of these two patterns:

Pattern One: **SV**   **Group B Connector**   **SV. (no comma)**

Pattern Two: **Group B Connector**   **SV,**   **SV.**

Exceptions:

     1)   Commas are optional in short sentences that start with Group B connectors (Pattern Two).

     2)   Some Group B connectors only work with Pattern One.

     3)   Sometimes a Pattern One sentence may have a comma for emphasis.

The following sentences are examples of basic complex sentences.

Pattern One: **SV**   **Group B Connector**   **SV.**

Example 1.

Patris felt relaxed because she had just returned from a restful vacation.

Example 2.

I finished the test early although it was not easy.

Example 3.

Students can study in the library whenever they have a break between classes.

Example 4.

We ordered the pizza after they arrived.

Example 5.

My family is more protective than some families are.

Pattern Two: **Group B Connector**   **SV,**   **SV.**

Example 1.

Because Patris had just returned from a restful vacation, she felt relaxed.

Example 2.

Although it was not easy, I finished the test early.

Example 3.

Whenever they have a break between classes, students can study in the library.

Example 4.

After they arrived we ordered the pizza. (Because this sentence is so short, a comma is optional.)

The Group B connector *than* cannot be used with Pattern Two.

Advanced Compound Sentences

An *advanced compound sentence* has at least two clauses connected by a *semicolon* alone or by an *adverbial conjunction* (also called a *conjunctive adverb*). In this book, we will refer to these words as "Group C Connectors." There are more than 15 of these connectors, including those listed below. Some Group C connectors consist of more than one word.

Adverbial Conjunctions (Group C Connectors)

also	as a result	consequently
furthermore	however	in addition
in contrast	instead	moreover
nevertheless	on the other hand	otherwise
then	therefore	thus

With very few exceptions, whenever these words are used to connect two clauses (SVs), they must follow one of the following two patterns:

Pattern One: **SV ;**   **Group C Connector,**   **SV.**

Pattern Two: **SV .**   **Group C Connector,**   **SV.**

Exceptions:

1)   A comma should not be used after the Group C word *then*.

2)   Some Group C connectors may also be used in the middle of a clause, with different punctuation, but then they are not considered as sentence connectors.

The following sentences are all advanced compound sentences. (Technically, Pattern Two consists of two simple sentences.)

Pattern One: **SV;**   **Group C Connector,**   **SV.**

Example 1.

We won our first four games; however, we lost the next three games straight.

Example 2.

The air was very warm; in contrast, the water was freezing!

Example 3.

> We enjoyed the food very much; moreover, the setting was beautiful.

Example 4.

> It is important to use sun block at the beach; otherwise, you could get a bad burn.

Example 5.

> There had been no rain for months; therefore, the trees were drying out.

Pattern Two: SV.   Group C,   SV.

Example 1.

> We won our first four games. However, we lost the next three games straight.

Example 2.

> The air was very warm. In contrast, the water was freezing!

Example 3.

> We enjoyed the food very much. Moreover, the setting was beautiful.

Example 4.

> It is important to use sun block at the beach. Otherwise, you could get a bad burn.

Example 5.

> There had been no rain for months. Therefore, the trees were drying out.

A Semicolon Alone

A semicolon alone can be used to join two clauses together. In order to use a semicolon alone, the second clause must be closely related in meaning to the first clause, and the meaning must be clear. For reasons of style, this pattern should not be overused.

Example:

> **SV   ;   SV.**

> We needed a break; we had worked all morning in the heat and high humidity.

Complex Sentences with Relative Clauses

This type of sentence has at least two clauses connected by a *relative pronoun* (that, which, who, whom, whose) or a *relative adverb* (where, when).

Relative clauses provide more information about the word they follow as well as connecting two clauses together. They are used in two patterns, with two variations, plus a special comma rule that tells whether to use commas or not.

The relative clauses are underlined in the examples below.

Pattern One: SV   **Relative Connector**   **SV.**

Example 1:

I read the book <u>that my teacher recommended</u>.

Variation One: The relative connector is the subject of the relative clause:

SV   <u>**Relative Connector=S**   **V.**</u>

Example 2:

She met the artist <u>who had painted her favorite picture</u>.

Variation Two: The relative connector can sometimes be left out, but only if the meaning is clear without it and the sentence feels natural.

SV   ~~**Relative Connector**~~   <u>**SV.**</u>

Example 3:

I read the book   ~~(that)~~ my teacher recommended.

Pattern Two: **S**   <u>**Relative Connector**</u>   <u>**SV**</u>   **V.**

Example 4:

The meal <u>that we prepared</u> was delicious.

Variation One: The relative connector is the subject of the relative clause:

S   <u>**Relative Connector =SV**</u>   **V.**

Example 5:

The artist <u>who painted murals</u> was there.

Variation Two: The relative connector can sometimes be left out, but only if the meaning is clear without it and the sentence feels natural.

S   <u>**Relative Connector**</u>   <u>**SV**</u>   **V.**

Example 6:

The meal   ~~(that)~~ <u>we prepared</u> was delicious.

Special Rule for Using Commas with Relative Clauses

If the relative clause is *essential* (necessary in order to identify the word it relates to), <u>don't use commas</u>. On the other hand, if the relative clause is *nonessential* (not necessary in order to identify the word it relates to), then <u>use commas</u>.

Example 7:

Leticia, <u>who needed only one more unit to graduate</u>, registered for classes last week.

In Example 7, the subject (Leticia) is already identified by name, which means the relative clause is *nonessential* to identify her, so we *use commas*.

Example 8:

The student <u>who always arrives early</u> was sick today.

In Example 8, the relative clause is *essential* to help identify the person it relates to, that is, to tell us which student it refers to. That's why we *don't use commas* in this sentence.

Avoiding Common Sentence Errors: Fragments, Run-On Sentences, and Comma Splices

Fragments

Fragments are incomplete sentences. Some fragments do not contain a complete clause with a subject and a verb, like Incorrect Example 1 below. Other fragments include a complete clause and only part of another one, like Incorrect Example 2.

Incorrect Example 1:

Working in the hot sun all day.

Incorrect Example 2:

Because John worked in the hot sun all day.

Incorrect Example 2 is incomplete because it contains the Group B sentence connector _because_ but no second clause to connect to.

Corrected Example 1:

Working in the hot sun all day <u>gave me a big appetite</u>.

Corrected Example 2:

> Because John worked in the hot sun all day, <u>he was tired</u>.

Run-On Sentences

Run-on sentences consist of two clauses without a correct sentence connector.

Incorrect Example 3:

> John was tired he worked in the hot sun all day.

This is a *run-on sentence* because it contains two clauses without a sentence connector:

Clause 1)   *John was tired*

Clause 2)   *He worked in the hot sun all day.*

Corrected Example 3:

> *After* John worked in the hot sun all day, he was tired.

OR   John was tired *because* he worked in the hot sun all day.

OR   John worked in the hot sun all day, *so* he was tired.

There are often several ways to connect two clauses correctly. The important thing is to add a correct connector (Group A,

Group B, Group C, or a Relative Connector) that sounds natural, expresses the correct meaning, and is correctly punctuated.

Comma Splices

Comma splices consist of two clauses that are connected only by a comma. In correct English, a comma is not enough to connect two clauses together.

Incorrect Example 4:

John was tired, he worked in the hot sun all day.

This is a *comma splice* because it connects two clauses (John was tired) and (he worked in the hot sun all day) with only a comma. Comma splices can be corrected the same way as run-on sentences. See the corrected examples above, under "Run-on Sentences."

Example Questions: Avoiding Common Sentence Errors

Directions: Choose the best substitute for the following sentence. If the sentence is already correct, choose "Leave as is."

Example 1:

Before the hot golden sun rose, Latisha was working in the garden.

A   Before the hot golden sun rose Latisha was working in the garden.

B   Before, the hot golden sun rose Latisha was working in the garden.

C   Before the hot golden sun risen, Latisha was working in the garden.

D   "Leave as is."

This sentence contains the Group B connector "before" using Pattern Two, so we need a comma before the second clause. Answer A does not have a comma. Answer B has the comma in the wrong place. Answer C contains an incomplete form of the verb. Only D is correct: "Leave as is."

Example 2:

Students, parents, and people of all ages in the school talent show.

A   Students, parents, and people of all ages including in the school talent show.

B   Students, parents, and people of all ages are in the school talent show.

C   Students, parents, and people of all ages included in the school talent show.

D   "Leave as is."

The original version is a fragment because it does not include a verb at all. Answers A and C do not use complete verbs, so they are fragments too. B is the best answer because it includes a complete verb and it makes sense.

Summary of Sentence Punctuation

Sentences consist of one or more *clauses*. Remember that a clause is a group of words that contains a complete subject and verb combination. Sentences with only one clause are called simple sentences. If a sentence includes more than one clause, the clauses must be connected correctly by a sentence connector (Group A, Group B, Group C, or Relative Connector), or sometimes by a semicolon alone.

Sentence Patterns

The following patterns are the most common in English. There are a few other patterns that are not as common, but you probably won't need any of them on the CAHSEE. The variations and exceptions are not on this list, but you can review them in the earlier part of this chapter.

1.   **SV**   **.**   **SV.**   **(simple sentences)**

2.   **SV**   **;**   **SV.**

3.   **SV**   **,**   **Group A**   **SV.**

4.   **SV   Group B   SV.**

5.   **Group B   SV,   SV.**

6.   **SV;   Group C,   SV.**

7.   **SV.   Group C ,   SV.   (simple sentences)**

8.   **SV   <u>Relative Connector</u>   SV.**
       (with or without a comma)

9.   **S   <u>Relative Connector</u>   SV   V.**
       (with or without commas)

Directions:

Choose the word or phrase that best completes the sentence.

Example Question 1:

Derek was refreshed after spending the week at a camp by the beautiful blue _____   he could come back the next year.

A   ocean**,** he hoped

B   ocean**;** he hoped

C   ocean and he hoped

D   ocean consequently he hoped

Answer A is a comma splice, and Answers C and D are run-on sentences. B is the best answer because it follows one of the correct sentence patterns: a semicolon alone.

Example Question 2:

Coyotes howled all night _____ the tired campers slept through it all.

A   long however

B   long, however

C   long; however,

D   long, however;

However is a Group C connector, so it needs a semicolon or period before it and a comma after it. C is the only answer that matches a correct Group C pattern.

More About Sentences

There are three other important sentence features which may be on the CAHSEE. These include the following:

- Phrases

- Placement of Modifiers

- Parallel Structure

Phrases

A *phrase* is a group of words that does not include a complete subject and verb. Phrases are useful for providing specific information, including time, place, manner, and other information, and can improve your score on the essay writing portion of the CAHSEE by making your writing richer and more detailed. Because phrases are not complete sentences by themselves, be sure to use them inside of a sentence, and not alone.

Here are a few examples of phrases that show time, place, manner, or other information.

Phrases

Time	Place	Manner	Other
at noon	by the clock tower	with a happy grin	with his friends
on Sunday	on the beach	gracefully and calmly	hoping to return
later today	resting at home	working hard	repaired and ready

When you write the short essay on the CAHSEE, be sure that your writing includes some phrases that show time, place, manner, or other specific information.

Placement of Modifiers

Phrases that provide useful information are sometimes called modifiers. They are usually placed right next to the nouns they modify or describe, as in the following examples where the modifiers are underlined:

Example 1:

Mowing his lawn, Jake found a snake.

Example 2:

Jake found a snake <u>hiding in the tall grass</u>.

In Example 1, "Mowing his lawn" describes what Jake is doing, so it is placed next to *Jake*. In Example 2, "hiding in the tall grass" describes what the snake is doing, so it is placed next to the word *snake*.

If you placed these modifiers in the wrong place, they would not make sense:

<u>Incorrect</u> *Example 1:*

Jake found a snake mowing his lawn.

<u>Incorrect</u> *Example 2:*

Hiding in the tall grass, Jake found a snake.

In these incorrect examples, it sounds like the snake was mowing the lawn and Jake was hiding in the tall grass!

It is very important to place modifiers in the right place, where they make sense.

Example Question:

Choose the best substitute for the following sentence. If the sentence is already correct, choose "Leave as is."

A bee stung Loralyn while cleaning her attic.

A   While cleaning her attic, a bee stung Loralyn.

B   A bee cleaning her attic stung Loralyn.

C   While cleaning her attic, Loralyn was stung by a bee.

D   "Leave as is."

Answer C is the best one. The other sentences seem to say that the bee was cleaning Loralyn's attic!

Parallel Structure

Parallel structure means using similar grammar and wording to show similar information. When a sentence contains more than one piece of information about someone or something, the information is often written using *parallel* structure.

In the following examples, the parallel items are underlined.

Example 1:

Patrick rested after he finished <u>cleaning the house</u>, <u>shopping for groceries</u>, and <u>reading his email</u>.

Example 1 includes a series of words ending in *-ing* that show three activities Patrick has finished doing. This is an example of correct parallel structure.

Example 2:

> Patrick rested after he had <u>cleaned the house</u>, <u>shopped for groceries</u>, and <u>answered his emails</u>.

Example 2 is also correct because it contains a series of *past participles* that show three activities that Patrick had already accomplished. However, if different types of grammatical structures are used in the same list, such as *-ing* words mixed in with past participles, the sentence will not be parallel.

<u>Incorrect</u> *Example 1:*

> Patrick was happy because he finished <u>cleaning the house</u>, <u>shopped for groceries</u>, and <u>returning his calls</u>.

Incorrect Example 1 has two *-ing* verbs and one past participle in the series of actions. It is not a correct sentence because it does not have parallel structure.

It is also important to be sure that the sentence makes sense and sounds logical. Otherwise, it will not be correct even if it has parallel structure.

Example Question:

Choose the best substitute for the following sentence. If the sentence is already correct, choose "Leave as is."

> **At camp last summer, Antonio learned to respect wildlife, clean up after himself, and get along with a whole cabin full of boys.**

A At camp last summer, Antonio learned to respect wildlife, cleaning up after himself, and get along with a whole cabin full of boys.

B At camp last summer, Antonio learned respecting wildlife, cleaning up after himself, and getting along with a whole cabin full of boys.

C At camp last summer, Antonio learned to respect wildlife, to clean up after himself, and get along with a whole cabin full of boys.

D "Leave as is."

Answer A has a series that is not parallel, with one *-ing* ending: *respect, cleaning, get along*. Answer B is parallel (respecting, cleaning, getting), but the grammar is not correct. Answer C is not parallel, with two infinitives and one simple form: *to respect, to clean*, and *get along*. The best answer is D, "Leave as is." The sentence is already parallel and correct, with a series of three simple verb forms after *to*: *respect, clean*, and *get along*.

Another possible correct answer might include a series of infinitive verbs that start with "to": *to respect, to clean*, and *to get along*.

Grammar and Usage

Grammar means using the correct forms and placement of words in sentences. This chapter contains a review of the following grammar topics:

- Verb Tense

- Subject and Verb Agreement

- Adjectives and Adverbs

- Pronouns

Verb Tense

The CAHSEE exam may ask some questions that require you to identify whether a verb is in the *past*, *present*, or *future* time. Reviewing the following verb tenses can help you do well on this type of question.

Verb Forms that Show Past Time

Some verb forms show that an action or condition happened in the past. The following are examples of these tenses and forms:

The children *went* to the park.

John *finished* his assignment.

We *didn't arrive* late yesterday morning.

He *couldn't help* us.

We *weren't paying* close enough attention.

She *was beginning* a new exercise program.

I *haven't had* breakfast yet.

She *has worked* here for three years.

No one *had remembered* to buy milk at the store.

Verb Forms that Show Present Time

Examples of verb forms that show that an action takes place or that a condition is true at the present time include the following:

We *can* always *count* on you when we *need* help.

Bill *works* five days a week.

I *work* every day.

She *doesn't like* to play tennis.

I *do not have* any time to waste.

I *am enjoying* this meal.

Antonio *is working* hard right now.

They are *not doing* what they should be.

Verb Forms that Show Future Time

Future time can be shown by a number of different verb forms and tenses. Here are some examples:

We *will get back* to you tomorrow.

They *won't be* disappointed with the quality of our work.

He *is going to travel* next summer.

I *am working* tomorrow night.

We *can help* you later today.

The plane from Los Angeles *leaves* at 6:17.

Our train *doesn't depart* until 7:00.

Example Question:

Directions: Choose the word or phrase that best completes the sentence.

We _____ for our math class later tonight, and we can't come over until we finish our homework.

A   were studying

B   don't study

C   have studied

D   will study

We know that the answer needs to show future time because the sentence says "later tonight," so the best answer is D.

Subject and Verb Agreement

In every sentence, each verb must *agree* with its *subject*. For example, <u>he *has*</u>, but <u>we *have*</u>. English has three categories of verbs for *subject and verb agreement* in the present tense: *most verbs*, *modal auxiliary verbs*, and the verb *"to be,"* which is in a category by itself.

In the past tense, only the verb *"to be"* has more than one form (*was*, *were*) and therefore must also *agree* with its subject.

(For a definition of subjects and verbs, see "Identifying Subjects and Verbs" in Chapter 5.)

Most Verbs

The *present tense* of most verbs consists of <u>two</u> forms. The first form is often called the *simple form* of the verb, and does not have a special ending. Examples include *play*, *go*, *wish*, *study*, etc. The simple form is used for all subjects except for *third-person singular* subjects, which have an *-s* ending (*plays*, *goes*, *wishes*, etc.).

In grammar, the term *first person* means the person who is writing or speaking or any group that he or she is included in: *I* or *we*. The *second person* is the reader(s) or listener(s): one of *you*, two of *you*, many of *you*. The *third person* is anyone or anything other than the speaker or listener: *they*, *he*, *she*, or *it*.

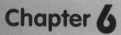

Only third person singular subjects use the *-s* ending—all other subjects use the simple form of the verb. The following chart has several examples.

Present Tense Subject and Verb Agreement

I, you, we, they (simple form)	he, she, it (*-s* ending)
own	owns
work	works
need	needs
plan	plans
go	goes
do	does
wish	wishes
match	matches
have	has

Most of these verbs just add *-s* with *he*, *she*, or *it*. Only one of these verbs has an irregular spelling in the present tense: *have/has*. There is also a spelling rule for the *-s* ending: Verbs that end with *-o*, *-s*, *-x*, *-z*, *-ch*, or *-sh* end in *-es* instead of just *-s*.

Modal Verbs

A few helping verbs have only <u>one</u> form for all subjects. These are called *modal auxiliary verbs*, and include *can*, *could*, *will*, *would*, *shall*, *should*, *may*, *might*, *must*, and *ought to*. After any of these modal verbs, the main verb is always in the simple form—there is no *-s* ending with these verbs.

Examples:

> I <u>will help</u> you with your homework if you help me with my car.

> He <u>can work</u> late tomorrow if his shift supervisor gives his approval.

> You <u>should plan</u> your time carefully.

> She <u>ought to plan</u> her time more carefully.

The Verb "To Be"

There is one verb that is completely irregular in the present tense: the verb *to be*. It is the only verb that has three forms in the present tense or two forms in the past tense.

Present Tense of "To Be"

I	we, you, they	he, she it
am	are	is

Examples:

- I <u>am</u> certain that your application has been received.

- They <u>are</u> ready to take the test.

- My book <u>is</u> used, but it <u>is</u> still in good shape.

Past Tense of "To Be"

I, he, she, it	we, you, they
was	were

Examples:

• Marta <u>was</u> certain that her father had finished washing the car.

• The boys <u>were</u> certain that they would finish their school project before the weekend.

Adjectives and Adverbs

Adjectives and *adverbs* are words that affect the meaning of other words. They provide specific information, including size, shape, manner, origin, quality, color, sound, intensity, and many other details.

Topics covered in this section include the following:

• Introduction to Descriptive Adjectives

• Introduction to Adverbs

• Comparative Adjectives and Adverbs

• Superlative Adjectives and Adverbs

• Participial Adjectives

Introduction to Descriptive Adjectives

Descriptive adjectives are words that are used to describe *nouns*—people, places, things, ideas, or animals. They usually come before the noun they describe: The acrobatic (*adjective*) dancers (*noun*) put on an entertaining show. Descriptive adjectives give valuable information about the nouns they describe.

The descriptive adjectives are <u>underlined</u> in the following examples:

Example 1.

The <u>dry</u> leaf hung from the <u>torn</u> spiderweb.

Example 2.

Anna used a <u>yellow</u> piece of paper to mark her* place in the book.

*For more information about *possessive adjectives* such as *her* in Example 2, see the section on *pronouns* later in this chapter.

Descriptive adjectives may also follow a linking verb such as a form of "to be":

Example 3.

Both of her brothers are <u>tall</u>.

Introduction to Adverbs

There are several types of *adverbs*. Most adverbs affect the meaning of action *verbs*. They may come at the beginning of a clause, before or after the verb, or sometimes at the end of the clause.

Most Adverbs

Most adverbs are formed by adding *-ly* to the corresponding adjective, as in the chart below. There are also two spelling rules, listed below the chart.

Adjectives and Adverbs

Adjective	Adverb
calm	calmly
sad	sadly
happy	happily
quiet	quietly
disgusted	disgustedly
fantastic	fantastically
cruel	cruelly

The spelling rules include the following:

1)   Add *-ally* (instead of *-ly*) to most adjectives that end with *-ic*, such as *fantastically* in the chart above

2)   After a consonant, change the final *-y* to *-i* before adding *-ly*, such as *happily* in the chart above.

In the examples below, the adverbs show the manner in which the subject (*he*) snuck into the kitchen.

Examples (adverbs are italicized):

Example 1.

> *Quietly* and *carefully*, he snuck into the kitchen for a midnight snack.

Example 2.

> He *quietly* snuck into the kitchen for a midnight snack.

Example 3.

> He snuck *quietly* into the kitchen for a midnight snack.

Example 4.

> He snuck into the kitchen for a midnight snack, *quietly* and *carefully*.

Irregular Adverbs

A few adverbs have irregular forms. These include the following:

Irregular Adverbs

Adjective	Adverb
good	well
hard	hard
fast	fast
early	early

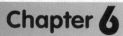

Adverbs of Place and Time

Adverbs that show *place* and *time* are often not formed from adjectives at all. These include such time words as *before*, *after*, *yesterday*, *tomorrow*, and place words like *left, right, forward*, and many more.

Example 5.

We finished painting the house *yesterday*.

Example 6.

They had obviously worked on boats *before*.

Example 7.

She turned *left* at the traffic signal.

Intensifiers

Other adverbs, also called *intensifiers*, affect the meaning of an adjective or another adverb. These include *very*, *quite*, *extremely*, *rather*, *somewhat*, and others.

Example 8.

He snuck into the kitchen for a midnight snack, *very* quietly and carefully.

Example 9.

She was *extremely* happy to learn that she had passed the test.

Another category of adverbs is used to join sentences together. For information about these *conjunctive adverbs,* also called *adverbial conjunctions*, see Chapter 5.

Comparative Adjectives and Adverbs

Some adjectives and adverbs can be used to *compare* two or more things. For example, in land area, Texas is *bigger* than California. On the other hand, California is *more populous* than Texas.

Comparative adjectives can have either of two forms, depending on how many syllables the adjective has. There are some irregular forms too.

The "-er" Ending

To form the comparative of adjectives of only one syllable, add *-er* to the original adjective. For example, tall → *taller;* fast → *faster.* Two-syllable adjectives that end in *-y* also end in *-er.*

Three spelling rules apply as well:

Spelling Rules for the *-er* Ending

1. If the adjective ends with a consonant, a vowel, and a consonant, double the final consonant before adding *-er.* For example, big → *bigger;* hot → *hotter.*

2. If the adjective ends with a silent *-e,* just add *-r.* For example, nice → *nicer;* fine → *finer.*

3. To form the comparative of two-syllable adjectives that end with *-y*, change the *-y* to *-i* and add *-er*: happy → *happier*, flimsy → *flimsier*.

More Than

To form the comparative of adjectives with three or more syllables, use *more* plus the adjective: *more interesting, more enlightening, more fascinating.* Also, the comparative of two-syllable adjectives that don't end in *-y* is usually formed this way: *more honest, more modest, more helpful.* A few adjectives can be used either way: *friendlier, more friendly.*

Irregular Comparative Adjectives

There are a few comparative adjectives that are not formed by adding *-er* or *more*. These include the following:

Irregular Comparative Adjectives

Adjective	Comparative adjective
good	better
well (meaning *healthy*)	better
bad	worse
far	farther (shows physical distance)
	further (additionally, more extended)

Comparative Adverbs

The *comparative* form of adverbs that end in *-ly* is usually made by using *more* plus the adverb.

Example 1.

Our team played *more defensively* in the second half.

The comparative form of short irregular adverbs is formed by adding *-er*.

Example 2.

My favorite class always seems to end *sooner* than the other classes.

A few adverbs can be used with either form, *-er* or *more*.

Example 3.

The turtles moved *more slowly* than the other animals.

OR

The turtles moved *slower* than the other animals.

Superlative Adjectives and Adverbs

While comparative adjectives are used to compare two or more things, *superlative* adjectives show that something is <u>unique</u>, <u>stands out</u>, or in some way is <u>more extreme than all of the others</u> in its group.

Notice the difference in the following example sentences:

Chapter 6

Example 1.   (comparative adjective)

John is *taller than* his brother Pete.

Example 2.   (superlative adjective)

John is *the tallest* person in his family.

The "-est" Ending

The superlative form of short adjectives of only one syllable is formed by adding *-est* to the original adjective, with the same three spelling rules as for the *-er* ending. For example, tall → *tallest*; big → *biggest*; fast → *fastest*; nice → *nicest*; happy → *happiest*; flimsy → *flimsiest*.

Most

To form the *superlative* of adjectives with three or more syllables, use *most* plus the adjective: *most interesting*, *most enlightening*, *most fascinating*.

The superlative of two-syllable adjectives that don't end in *-y* is also usually formed with *most* plus the adjective: *most honest*, *most modest*, *most helpful*. A few adjectives can be used either way: *most friendly*, *friendliest*.

Irregular Superlative Adjectives

There are a few superlative adjectives that are not formed by adding *-est* or *most*. These include the following:

Irregular Superlative Adjectives

Adjective	Superlative Adjective
good	best
bad	worst
far	farthest (shows physical distance)
	furthest (additionally, more extended)

Directions:

Choose the answer that best completes the sentence.

Example Question 1.

"Which of these three cars gets the _____ mileage?" the car buyer asked the salesperson.

A goodest

B best

C bestest

D better

The answer to this question needs to be a superlative rather than a comparative because we want to know which car stands out from the others. D is a comparative form, and A and C ("goodest" and "bestest") are incorrect forms. B is the best answer because it is the only correct superlative form.

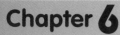

Example Question 2.

Sociology is the _____ of all my classes.

    A   interesting

    B   more interesting

    C   most interesting

    D   most interestingly

The answer to Example 2 needs to be a *superlative adjective* because we are looking for the class that stands out from the rest rather than comparing two classes. Answer C is the only superlative adjective.

Superlative Adverbs

The *superlative* form of adverbs that end in *-ly* is usually made by using *the most* plus the adverb.

Participial Adjectives

The *present participle* (the *-ing* form) and the *past participle* of many verbs can also be used as adjectives. *Present participles* show that the noun is active, and *past participles* show that the noun receives the action portrayed by the verb. (For more information on active and passive constructions, see the section on using the active voice in Chapter 4.)

The following example sentences show *present participles* used as adjectives (in *italics*):

Example 1.

The *rocking* boat soon put us to sleep.

Example 2.

Hanging from the tree, the zoo monkey made faces at the *visiting* schoolchildren.

The following example sentences show *past participles* used as adjectives (in italics):

Example 3.

Their chores *done*, the children bounced energetically on the trampoline.

Example 4.

The *boiled* artichokes were an unusual treat for our picnic.

While there will probably not be a question about participial adjectives on the CAHSEE, they are useful tools to make your writing more descriptive, which can help you improve your score on the essay portion of the test.

Pronouns

Definition of Pronouns

A *pronoun* is a word that is used in place of a noun. This section of the book provides information on *personal pronouns* and *indefinite pronouns*.

Personal Pronouns

Questions on *personal pronouns* are often included on the CAHSEE. *Personal pronouns* include the following categories:

- Subject Pronouns

- Object Pronouns

- Possessive Adjectives

- Possessive Pronouns

- Reflexive (or Emphatic) Pronouns

The following chart will help you keep track of personal pronouns.

Personal Pronouns

Subject	Object	Possessive Adjective	Possessive Pronoun	Reflexive (or Emphatic)
I	me	my	mine	myself
we	us	our	ours	ourselves
you	you	your	yours	yourself
				yourselves
he	him	his	his	himself
she	her	her	hers	herself
it	it	its	∅	itself
they	them	their	theirs	themselves

Subject Pronouns

Subject pronouns are used as the subject of a clause or sentence, as underlined in the following examples:

Example 1.

They are working tomorrow afternoon.

Example 2.

I need a new car.

Example 3.

She is watching her favorite movie tonight.

Object Pronouns

In grammar terms, the *object* of a sentence is usually the person or thing that receives the action. *Object pronouns* are used as direct objects, indirect objects, or as the object of a preposition, as underlined in the following examples:

Example 4.

Their manager gave <u>them</u> their new assignments.

Example 5.

Not having a car worries <u>me</u>.

Example 6.

We asked <u>her</u> to bring her favorite movie.

Example 7.

They were speaking to <u>us</u>.

Be careful that you use subject and object pronouns correctly, especially when there is more than one pronoun, as in the following example sentences:

Example 8.

<u>He and I</u> picked up the tickets.

Example 9.

The box office held the tickets for <u>him and me</u>.

In sentences like Example 8, where the pronouns are the *subject* of the sentence, we must use *subject pronouns*. In sentences like Example 9, the pronouns are *objects* of a preposition (*for*), so object pronouns must be used.

Possessive Adjectives

Possessive <u>*adjectives*</u> are used *with a noun*, as underlined in the following examples:

Example 10.

<u>Their</u> manager gave them their new assignments.

Example 11.

<u>My</u> books were heavy.

Example 12.

We asked him to bring <u>his</u> favorite movie.

Possessive Pronouns

Possessive <u>*pronouns*</u> are used in place of a noun, as underlined in the following examples:

Example 13.

His car is in good shape, but <u>hers</u> needs some work.

(used in place of *her car*)

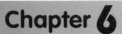

Example 14.

His backpack was heavy, but <u>mine</u> was lighter.

(used in place of *my backpack*)

Example 15.

They brought their favorite games, and we brought <u>ours</u>.

(used in place of *our favorite games*)

Example Question:

Choose the word or phrase that is the best answer to fill in the blank.

The audience applauded the band members and _____ conductor.

A   his

B   its

C   we

D   their

The correct answer is D, because it is the correct possessive adjective form for the noun *band members*.

Reflexive (or Emphatic) Pronouns

Reflexive pronouns are used when the subject of the sentence also receives the action, as in Examples 16 and 17. They can also be used to give stronger *emphasis* to the pronoun, as in Examples 18 and 19.

Example 16.

The bird fought many battles with <u>himself</u> in the mirror.

Example 17.

I hurt <u>myself</u> when I tripped over the curb.

Example 18.

The two-year-old girls were insistent that they could tie their shoes by <u>themselves</u>.

Example 19.

If you want something done right, you might have to do it <u>yourself</u>.

Notice that the pronoun *you* has two reflexive forms: *yourself* and *yourselves*. *Yourself* is used when you are speaking to only one person (*you* singular), and *yourselves* is used when you are addressing more than one person (*you* plural).

Example Question:

Choose the best word or phrase to fill in the blank.

Instead of tying the kindergarten children's shoelaces, the Teaching Assistant showed them how to do it _____.

A   themselves

B   ourselves

C   yourself

D   themself

The correct answer is A. The correct answer will reflect that the children (*they*) learned how to tie their own shoelaces. Answer B corresponds to *we,* and Answer C refers to *you.* Answer D is an incorrect form. The best answer is A, because *themselves* is the only reflexive pronoun that corresponds to *the children.*

Indefinite Pronouns

Indefinite pronouns are words that do not relate to specific people. Grammatically, some indefinite pronouns are considered to be singular rather than plural even when they represent more than one person. These include the following:

Singular Indefinite Pronouns

anybody	anyone
everybody	everyone
nobody	no one
somebody	someone
either	neither
each	every

Example 1.

> Everyone needs to dry off from the pool before coming into the house.

Example 2.

> Each of the three brothers has his own favorite basketball lay-up.

Example 3. (Incorrect)

> Each student needs to bring their own pen and paper.

Corrected Example 3.

> Each student needs to bring his or her own pen and paper.

Notice that in the three examples above, the indefinite pronouns *everyone* and *each* require singular verb forms, *needs* and *has*, even though they refer to more than one person. (For a review of subjects and verbs, see Subject and Verb Agreement earlier in this chapter.)

In Incorrect Example 3, the pronoun *their* is plural, but *each* is singular, so the pronouns do not agree. "His or her" is correct because *his* and *her* are singular pronouns that agree with the subject "Each student."

Chapter

7

Punctuation

and

Capitalization

This chapter contains a review of the following topics:

- Titles of Publications

- Quotation Marks

- Apostrophes

- Commas

- Semicolons

- Colons

- Dashes

- Ellipses

- Capitalization

Titles of Publications

Books and Other Complete Works

With few exceptions, titles of publications, including books, magazines, journals, newspapers, television shows, and movies or videos, must be either <u>underlined</u> or *italicized*.

Examples:

Books

<u>Merriam-Webster's Desk Dictionary</u>

or *Merriam-Webster's Desk Dictionary*

<u>Gone with the Wind</u>

or *Gone with the Wind* (also a movie)

Newspapers

<u>USA Today</u>

or

USA Today

Magazines

National Geographic

or

National Geographic.

Articles, Chapters, Poems, Songs, etc.

Use quotation marks (" ") for titles of articles in magazines, journals, or newspapers, and for book chapters, readings in a collection, poems, songs, and other short pieces of writing that appear in a longer publication.

Examples:

Songs

"How Can It Be"

"Stand by Me"

Articles

"Hawaii Volcano Still Perking"

"How to Win the College Game"

Poems

"The Road Less Traveled"

"The Raven"

Example Question:

Choose the answer that best completes the sentence.

The titles of two popular news magazines are _____.

A   <u>Time</u> and <u>Newsweek</u>

B   "Time" and "Newsweek"

C   "<u>Time</u>" and "<u>Newsweek</u>"

D   Time and Newsweek

Quotation marks are used with titles of articles, but not whole magazines, so B and C are incorrect. Publications such as magazines must be either <u>underlined</u> or *italicized*, so A is the best answer.

Quotation Marks

Quotation marks are used in three main ways:

- To quote the exact words that someone wrote or said.

- To show that there is some doubt about the word in quotes.

- To indicate the title of an article or other short work.

The CAHSEE probably will not include questions about using quotation marks to show doubt about the word in quotes, and titles of publications are included in the previous section of this chapter. Therefore, this section will focus on using quotation marks to report the exact words that someone spoke or wrote.

Reporting Exact Words

Whenever you report the exact words that someone said or wrote, you must use *quotation marks*. The only exception is if the quotation is very long—more than four lines of text—in which case the entire quotation is indented instead of using quotation marks.

Reporting verbs such as *said*, *exclaimed*, *told*, *asked*, or *whispered* are often used to indicate a quotation. Reporting verbs can be before the quoted words, in the middle, or at the end, as in the following example sentences:

Example 1.

His attorney <u>told</u> the judge, "There is no basis for that accusation."

Example 2.

> "Alan and Lynn might be interested in singing in the play," <u>suggested</u> the drama teacher, "if they aren't too busy with the choir."

Example 3.

> "You are the first person to reach my cave in over 20 years," <u>whispered</u> the hermit.

Interrupted Quotations

Example 2 is an interrupted quotation, which means that the reporting words *suggested the drama teacher* are in the middle of the sentence being quoted instead of at the beginning or the end. Interrupted quotations need a comma and a quotation mark after the end of the first part of the quotation, then a comma after the reporting words, and another quotation mark at the beginning of the second section—exactly as in Example 2 above.

Periods, Commas, Question Marks, and Exclamation Marks with Quotations

Periods and commas are almost always placed ***inside of*** the quotation marks, as in each example above. However, question marks and exclamation marks can be placed either *inside* or *outside* of the quotation marks, depending on the structure and meaning of the sentence.

When the sentence being quoted is a question or exclamation, the question mark or exclamation mark goes <u>inside</u> of the quotation marks, as in the following example sentences:

Example 4.

The test question asked, "What were the causes of the American Civil War?"

Example 5.

Terri asked, "Do you understand the homework?"

Example 6.

She replied, "Never in a million years!"

However, if the question or exclamation is <u>not</u> part of the words being quoted, then the question mark or exclamation mark must go <u>outside</u> of the quotation marks:

Example 7.

What did John Kennedy mean when he said, "Ask not what your country can do for you"?

Example 8.

It was a mistake to tell my supervisor, "I can take on another project now"!

Example Question:

Which is the correct way to quote the following sentence?

One ought, every day at least, to hear a little song, read a good poem, see a fine picture, and if it were possible, to speak a few reasonable words.
             —Johann Wolfgang von Goethe

A   "One ought, every day at least, says Goethe, to hear a little song, read a good poem, see a fine picture, and if it were possible, to speak a few reasonable words."

B   "One ought, every day at least," says Goethe, "to hear a little song, read a good poem, see a fine picture, and if it were possible, to speak a few reasonable words."

C   One ought, every day at least, says Goethe, to hear a little song, read a good poem, see a fine picture, and if it were possible, to speak a few reasonable words.

D   "One ought, every day at least," says Goethe, to hear a little song, read a good poem, see a fine picture, and if it were possible, to speak a few reasonable words."

All of the words except for the reporting words *says Goethe* need to be inside of the quotation marks. Since this is an example of an interrupted quotation, the best answer is B.

Apostrophes

An apostrophe is a little symbol that looks a lot like a single quotation mark, or a comma that has been raised to the top of the line. For example, the word **can't** has an apostrophe between the **n** and the **t**. Apostrophes are used in three main situations:

- With *contractions:* words that have been shortened and combined

- With the possessive form of a noun

- To show the plural form of a number, a letter, or a symbol.

Apostrophes with Contractions

Shortened forms of words are called *contractions*. They have an apostrophe where one or more letters are missing. The following chart has just a few examples of the many contractions that are in common use.

Examples of Contractions

don't (do not)	shouldn't (should not)
she's (she is *or* she has)	I've (I have)
they'd (they would *or* they had)	dep't. *or* dept. (department)

Contractions are often used in *informal* writing. With *formal* writing such as the essay on the CAHSEE test, however, you should generally write out the complete words instead of using contractions (unless you are quoting someone who is speaking informally).

Apostrophes with Possessives

Apostrophes are also used with a *noun* (a *noun* is a person, place, thing, animal, or idea) to make it *possessive*—to show that it belongs to someone (or something) in some way.

Possessive Form of Most Nouns

To make the possessive form of a noun, we normally add an apostrophe and an **-s**, as in the following examples.

Possessives with Apostrophes

the <u>teacher's</u> explanation	the <u>store's</u> merchandise
<u>María's</u> new books.	<u>Bess's</u> friend Marvin
the <u>children's</u> choir.	our <u>dog's</u> dietary requirements

Possessive Form of Plural Nouns that End with -S

When the noun is plural and already ends in an **-s**, just add an apostrophe, as in the following examples:

- companies: the two **companies**' headquarters buildings

- animals: all of the zoo **animals**' cages

- teachers: my three **teachers**' opinions.

Possessive Form of Singular Nouns that End with -S

With singular nouns that end in **-s**, sometimes the possessive is formed with just an apostrophe, and sometimes it is formed with an apostrophe and another **-s**, depending on which way sounds best. Other times, the possessive is avoided completely, such as *bus driver* (not *bus's driver*), and *the cause of the mess* (not *the mess's cause*). You will probably not see a question about this specific point on the CAHSEE.

Special Uses of Apostrophes

The CAHSEE will probably not include the special uses of apostrophes, which some writers and publishers use to indicate the plural of numbers such as years (the 1920's, the 1800's) or letters, such as grades (straight A's). However, one of these uses of the apostrophe may come in handy on the writing portion of the test. If you use any apostrophes in your essay answers, remember to check to see that you have used them correctly.

Commas

The *comma* (**,**) is probably harder to learn than other punctuation marks because commas are used in several different situations. These situations can be divided into five main categories:

- With <u>Sentence Connectors</u>

- With <u>Extra Information</u>

- With <u>Introductory Elements</u>

- With <u>Items in a Series</u>

- In <u>Certain Special Cases</u> including *Times* and *Places*, or for reasons of *Style* or *Emphasis.*

Commas with Sentence Connectors

Commas are used in different ways with each different type of sentence connector. A short summary is listed below, but you should also refer back to the section on sentence connectors in Chapter 5 for a more detailed review of sentence structure.

Commas with Group A Connectors

With few exceptions, a comma is used before a Group A Connector (coordinating conjunction) used to connect two clauses.

Example 1.

The sun came out, *but* snow was still blowing in our faces.

Commas with Group B Connectors

When a sentence starts with a Group B Connector, a comma is used between the two clauses.

Example 2.

Because our feet were cold and wet from walking in the snow, we decided to get back in the van and change into dry socks and shoes.

Commas with Group C Connectors

With one exception, a comma is used after a Group C Connector used to connect two clauses.

Example 3.

We wanted to continue driving up the mountain road; *however*, we had forgotten to bring chains for driving on icy roads.

Commas with Extra Information

Another main use of commas is to show that some of the sentence is "extra," not really necessary, repeated information, an afterthought, or in some way less important than other information in the sentence. In addition to setting off nonessential relative clauses as mentioned in Chapter 5, commas may be used to set off other sorts of extra information anywhere in a sentence.

Commas with Relative Clauses

Commas are used before and after *nonessential relative clauses*—clauses that are not necessary for identification of the word they relate to. (See Chapter 5 for more examples and details about using commas with relative clauses.)

Example 4.

The Eilan Donan Castle, <u>where my family lived centuries ago,</u> is still impressive today.

Example 5.

Centuries ago my family lived in the Eilan Donan Castle, <u>which is still impressive today</u>.

Commas are <u>not</u> used with *essential* relative clauses (clauses that are necessary in order to identify the word they relate to).

Example 6.

The neighbor <u>who is building the new house</u> has almost finished the job. (no commas)

Commas with Appositives

An *appositive* is when a writer refers to the same person or thing in two different ways, one right after the other. In Example 8 below, "my brother's soccer coach" is an appositive that refers to Matt. Commas are used on both sides of appositives, almost as if they were parentheses "**( )**." (Parentheses would also be correct, but they are often not considered appropriate for formal writing such as most paragraphs and essays for academic classes.)

Example 7.

> Matt**,** <u>my brother's soccer coach</u>**,** encouraged him to improve his defensive skills.

Example 8.

> Our ancestral home**,** <u>the Eilan Donan castle</u>**,** is still impressive today.

Commas with Introductory Elements

Commas are very common after introductory elements—anything that comes before the subject and verb of the main clause, including times and places.

Example 9.

> <u>With excitement and some nervousness</u>**,** I approached the room where I would have my interview.

Example 10.

> <u>At 3:00 in the morning</u>**,** the meteor storm intensified.

Example 11.

> In the mountains, we need to be very watchful for sudden changes in the weather.

Commas with Items in a Series

Commas are used when three or more items are listed in a *series*.

Example 12.

> Shannon, Anna, and Genevieve came to my 16th birthday party.

Example 13.

> Rachel is studying literature, biology, psychology, and Old Testament at college this semester.

Commas in Certain Special Cases

Commas are often used in several special cases: with *dates*, with *place names*, with *addresses*, and for reasons of *style* or *emphasis*.

Commas with Dates

Commas are used with *dates* when they are written in a sentence.

Example 14.

> José is graduating from college on Friday, May 12, 2006.

Commas with Place Names

Commas are used when the names of a *city*, *county*, *region*, or *country* are used together in a sentence.

Example 15.

> The Plaza of the Three Cultures in Mexico City, Mexico, is one of the most famous landmarks in the area.

Commas with Addresses

Commas are also used with *addresses*. Do not use a comma before the zip code.

Example 16.

> You may write to the author at Southwestern College, 900 Otay Lakes Road, Chula Vista, CA 91977.

Commas for Style or Emphasis

A few of the comma rules above have some flexibility to allow for personal style. For example, some writers prefer to use a comma even when a sentence is fairly short, while others prefer not to use a comma in a short sentence like the one that follows.

Example 17.

> I worked until 7:00, and then I went grocery shopping.

> OR:

> I worked until 7:00 and then I went grocery shopping. (no comma)

Another optional use of the comma is to emphasize a contrast in a sentence. For example, the comma in the sentence below is not required with the sentence connector *although*. By including the comma, the writer emphasizes the contrast between the ideas in the first clause and the second clause.

Example 18.

> I was not worried about failing the test, although this would be my second try.

Semicolons

Even though *semicolons* (;) are not used as often as commas, they are useful in some sentences. There are three main uses of semicolons:

- To Join Two Clauses Together with Group C Sentence Connectors

- To Join Two Related Clauses Together with a Semicolon Alone

- To Separate Parts of a Sentence when there are commas inside one or more of the parts.

(For more information on specific uses of semicolons, check out the Powerpoint presentation on this website: http://webster.commnet.edu/grammar/marks/semicolon.htm.)

To Join Clauses Together

For complete information on joining two clauses together with a *semicolon alone* and a *semicolon with a Group C connector*, see Chapter 5. Remember that semicolons slow down the reader and make the writing seem quite formal, so they should be used only where appropriate.

To Separate Parts of a Sentence

The third use of semicolons is to *separate parts of a sentence* when there are commas inside one or more of the parts. A sentence with more than one series with commas can be confusing, unless each series is set off by semicolons instead of just commas.

In Incorrect Example 1 below, the writer visits three places, but it is difficult to know where one place leaves off and the next place begins because commas are used inside each part as well as between the parts:

Incorrect Example 1.

Last summer we visited Disneyland, in Anaheim, California, Avalon, on Catalina Island, just off the California coast, and the Grand Canyon, in northern Arizona.

In the corrected example below, semicolons are used to separate the parts of the sentence that show the three locations, making the sentence much easier to understand:

Corrected Example 1.

Last summer we visited Disneyland, in Anaheim, California; Avalon, on Catalina Island, just off the California coast; and the Grand Canyon, in northern Arizona.

Colons

A *colon* (:) can be used to introduce a list, an explanation, or a quotation. Colons must always follow a complete sentence.

To see more detailed information about using *colons*, see the following website: http://webster.commnet.edu/grammar/marks/colon.htm.

Using Colons to Introduce a List

Colons can be used to introduce a list after a complete sentence, as in Example 1:

Example 1.

<u>Even without a computer, a home study area can be very useful if you have the right tools</u>: a desk dictionary, a good reading lamp, a drawer or container for pens and markers, a supply of the right kind of paper, and a place to lay out your textbooks as you work with them.

Avoiding a Common Error with Colons

A colon should <u>not</u> be used to introduce a list that is a necessary part of a sentence, as in Example 2:

Example 2.

Even without a computer, a home study area can be very useful if you have a desk dictionary, a good reading lamp, a drawer or container for pens and markers, a supply of the right kind of paper, and a place to lay out your textbooks as you work with them.

In Example 2, the part of the sentence before the list, "Even without a computer, a home study area can be very useful if you have," would not be a complete sentence, so a colon is not used.

Incorrect Example 3 (below) shows the incorrect use of a colon.

Incorrect Example 3.

Last semester I took**:** biology, Spanish, computer networking, and modern dance.

Corrected Example 3.

Last semester I took biology, Spanish, computer networking, and modern dance.

OR:

Last semester I took four subjects**:** biology, Spanish, computer networking, and modern dance.

Using a Colon to Introduce a Quotation

In certain cases, a colon can be used to introduce a quotation.

Example 4.

The coach of the winning team made a request**:** "Please save your questions for the press conference."

Using a Colon to Introduce an Explanation

A colon may also be used to introduce an explanation or examples.

Example 5.

It is easy to see why their team won: They pitched better, hit more runs, and made fewer errors.

Dashes

Dashes (–) are used to call attention to something in a sentence. They are often considered to be more informal than commas, semicolons, or colons. While many writers use them effectively, the CAHSEE will probably not include any questions about them. Because they are considered to be informal, you should probably avoid using them in the essay that you write for the CAHSEE.

Ellipses

Ellipses (...) are used to show that words or an idea continue even though they are not stated, and are often found in quoted material. When they are used at the end of a sentence, they are followed by a period, making four "dots" in a row, or by an exclamation point or question mark.

Example 1:

> Our teacher told us specifically, "You need to have good attendance...if you want to do well in this class."

In Example 1, the ellipsis shows that the teacher said something else that was not included in the quotation.

Example 2:

> If I left the iron turned on when we left the house.... We need to go back and check, just to be sure.

In Example 2, the ellipsis is at the end of the first sentence, so it is followed by a period.

Capitalization

The CAHSEE will probably not ask you any questions about capitalization, but knowing when to capitalize words can help you get a better score on your essay.

The first word of every sentence, the pronoun "I", and proper nouns should be *capitalized*.

The First Word of a Sentence

Always capitalize the *first word of every sentence*, even sentences in quotes and sentences that follow colons.

Example 1.

Trees and plants improve the air quality.

Example 2.

Sarah said, "**T**oday is the hottest day in several years."

The Pronoun "I"

Capitalize the pronoun "*I*" but not the other personal pronouns.

Example 3.

The other students and **I** decided to surprise the teacher with better grades on our last test.

Proper Nouns

Capitalize *proper nouns*. These include the following:

- Names and titles of *specific people*: Mrs. Jaynes, David, Pastor Ernst, Professor Johnson. Capitalize words used as names: "Let's ask <u>Grandma</u> if she wants to go with us." Do not capitalize these words otherwise: "Is your <u>grandma</u> a real estate agent?"

- Names of *nationalities* and *ethnicities*, even when referring to things rather than people: Cajun food, Native American history.

- Names of *specific places* including businesses and buildings, streets, cities, states, countries, regions, continents, geographical features such as lakes, rivers, and mountains, and even planets, stars, and constellations: Speedy-Mart, the Hall of Justice, Bonita Rd., Chicago, New Jersey, Japan, Northern Europe, Africa, Lake Huron, the Amazon, Mount McKinley, Mars, Alpha Centauri, Orion.

- Names of *specific organizations* including teams, companies, and organizations: the Dodgers, Sprint, the Department of Homeland Security.

- Names of *specific days and months*, <u>but not the seasons</u>: Monday, June, Christmas, New Year's Day, <u>summer</u>.

- Words that relate to *religions, religious events*, and *holy books*: Catholic, the Resurrection, the Bible, the Koran.

- Names of *historical events and documents*: World War II, the Treaty of Guadalupe Hidalgo, the Renaissance.

- Names of *specific planes, trains, boats, and other vehicles that have their own names*: *Air Force One*, the *Orient Express*, *Voyager*. These names also need to be italicized or underlined.

- Key words in titles of publications, short works, and art works: *Time Magazine*, *Attack of the Killer Tomatoes*, "Jabberwocky," *The Thinker*. (See the section "Titles of Publications" at the beginning of this chapter to review which of these titles must also be italicized or underlined.)

CAHSEE
English-Language Arts

Section 4:
Essay Writing

The Steps
of the
Writing Process

This chapter describes the steps that you should follow to *begin*, *organize*, *write*, and *check* your essay. These steps are very similar for all of the different types of essays that you will be asked to write.

Are you one of the many people who feel anxious or who get a mental blank when you have to write an essay? If so, take a minute to stretch and relax before you start to write the CAHSEE essay, and then remind yourself of the steps of the writing process before you start to write the essay. The steps are listed below, and the rest of this chapter explains each step in more detail.

Outline of Instructions for Writing an Essay

I. Understanding the Assigned Topic

II. Prewriting

- Get ideas onto the paper

- Organize the information

III. Writing

- Write a thesis statement

- Support the thesis statement with key points

- Include supporting information

- Use transition sentences between key points

- Write a conclusion

IV. Revising

- Check for completeness and organization

- Check to see that the essay reads smoothly

- Correct mistakes in sentences, grammar, spelling, and punctuation

Step-by-Step Instructions for Writing an Essay

I.   Understanding the Assigned Topic

Read the test prompt carefully for the answer to these questions:

1.   What *type* of essay do I need to write? and

2.   *Exactly* what topic is the test prompt asking me to write on?

II.   Prewriting

Get Ideas Onto the Paper

A very important step in the writing process that people sometimes overlook is to use a *prewriting technique* such as *brainstorming*, *freewriting*, or *diagramming* to get some ideas down on scratch paper so that you have something to work with as you write your essay. Different people prefer different prewriting techniques, so it would be a good idea to try out these techniques before the test. That way you will already know which techniques work best for you.

Another helpful prewriting approach not covered in this book can be found at Purdue University's Online Writing Lab, available online at http://owl.english.purdue.edu/handouts/ general/gl_plan2.html.

Brainstorming

The first technique, *brainstorming,* means writing down everything related to the topic that comes into your mind. On a piece of scrap paper, write down words, expressions, notes, sentences, and in general, whatever occurs to you. This is not the time to worry about organization, grammar, spelling, or punctuation—you will have time to check those important details in the following steps.

Freewriting

Freewriting is another prewriting technique that many writers find useful to help them get ideas on paper. Start writing about your topic in complete sentences, just as the ideas come into your mind. Again, do not worry about the organization of the essay, or about any of the editing details (grammar, spelling, or punctuation) at this step. Just write down everything you can think of.

Diagramming

Diagramming is another useful prewriting technique for discovering ideas. Write the topic in the middle of the page, and draw lines out from there (some people draw a circle around the topic). At the end of each line, write different points about the topic, as soon as you think of them. As you add more details, write them close to other points that they relate to, and draw lines to connect them to those points. The end result looks something like a spider web, or a circle with lines going out from it.

Organize the Information

After you have done some prewriting and written some raw information about your topic down on scratch paper, the next step is to *organize the information*. One way to do this is to circle similar ideas from your prewriting, and draw lines to connect them together into clusters or main points. For example, if your topic is to write about an important event in history, such as the Roman occupation of Judah, you might notice that several of your prewriting points relate to a similar subtopic, maybe the role of the Zealot movement or the siege of Masada.

By drawing a line between these points, you will be able to include all of them when you start writing about that topic. Each group of connected points can become one major part of your essay, which will make the essay much easier to write.

As you are organizing your information you may discover that you need more information. If you think of some additional information that you can use in your paper, write those ideas down on the paper too. When you have an idea of how your essay should be organized, the next step is to start writing the actual essay. (For more detailed information about each part of an essay, see Chapter 9.)

III. Writing

Write a Thesis Statement

As you start to organize the information you came up with in your prewriting activity, be thinking about the main idea that you want to communicate. Write this main idea, or thesis, in one or two sentences, on a clean piece of scratch paper. This will be your *thesis statement.*

Support the Thesis Statement with Key Points

After you have written the thesis statement, decide on your *key points*. These are the major points that support your thesis statement. If your essay is long enough, each key point will be in its own paragraph.

You may already have decided on your key points when you organized the information in your prewriting activity. However, if your key points do not cover all that you want to say, or if one of your key points does not relate to the thesis statement, you may need to add or delete a key point or two.

Include Supporting Information

Each of your key points needs *supporting information.* This can include various details, examples, or other points. In your prewriting, this is the information that you grouped together into clusters. If one or more of your key points needs more details, add some. If you have too many details about one or more of your key points, you will need to cut some out of your final essay, or reorganize the key points.

Use Transition Sentences Between Key Points

As you finish writing about each key point, you may want to write a *transition sentence* to connect it smoothly to the next key point. This will make your paper flow smoothly and help the readers follow what you are trying to tell them.

Write a Conclusion

At the end of your essay, you will need to write a *conclusion*—one or more sentences that make the paper feel finished. You may wish to choose one of the following techniques:

- Restate the thesis statement using different words

- Tell the importance of the material in the essay

- Emphasize a lesson contained in the essay (if there is one)

- Look to the future (preview what happens *after* the events in the essay)

- Use anything else that makes the essay feel finished.

More information about writing a conclusion is included in Chapter 9.

IV. Revising

Check for Completeness and Organization

In a test situation such as the CAHSEE, you may not have much time to revise your paper. However, it is important that you read it over carefully to be sure that your essay is complete, with a thesis statement, main points, support, transitions, and a conclusion. Also check to be sure that the meaning is clear and that your key points support your main idea—your *thesis*.

Check to See that the Essay Reads Smoothly

After you have checked to see that your essay communicates what you want it to say, ask yourself if it reads smoothly. If the key points are not connected smoothly, add one or more transitions and read it again.

Correct Mistakes in Sentences, Grammar, Spelling, and Punctuation

The final step in revising your essay is very important. You need to check your sentences, grammar, spelling, and punctuation. Look for the kinds of errors that you have made on other writing assignments in the past. For example, if you sometimes have problems with commas, or with the past tense, or with run-on sentences, look carefully for that kind of error.

When you find an error, correct it, and when you have checked everything, carefully write a clean copy of the essay in the space provided on the answer sheet. Request additional paper if you need it. Also remember that you can ask for more time if you need it.

(See Chapters 5, 6, and 7 for specific information about sentences, grammar and usage, and spelling, punctuation, and capitalization.)

Essay
Structure

Chapter 8 focused on the *steps* of writing an essay, while this chapter focuses on the individual parts, or *elements*, of an essay.

Each essay needs to have a beginning, a middle, and an end, otherwise known as the *introduction*, *body*, and *conclusion*. Usually, each of these parts will consist of at least one *paragraph*, and the body may consist of several paragraphs. All the parts of the essay have to work together to support the main idea, or thesis.

There are many different types of essays, but they all share the same important parts. Keeping the elements of an effective essay in mind will help you write your essay for the CAHSEE.

The Introduction

The *introduction* is the first paragraph (or sometimes the first two paragraphs) of the essay. It serves two purposes: to get the reader interested in the topic of the essay, and to tell the reader what the essay is all about—the main idea, or *thesis*.

Introductory Sentences

The first one or two sentences of the introduction are usually introductory sentences that try to "hook" the reader into wanting to read the rest of the essay. Some effective strategies to accomplish this are to provide *background information*, *interesting details*, *a benefit to the reader*, or a statement as to *why the topic is important*.

For example, if you are asked to write a business letter, specifically a letter of application for a job, you would probably write an introductory statement to get the readers interested, as in the following example:

Example Introductory Sentence

This is a letter of application for the position of chemistry lab assistant at Sandusky College.

This introduction immediately tells the readers what they want to know: the purpose of the letter.

Thesis Statement (Main Idea Statement)

The second part of the introduction is usually the *thesis statement*, or the main idea statement, for the whole essay. (For more information about the main idea of a reading or essay, refer back to Chapter 2.) The thesis statement clearly states the topic of the essay. It is usually one sentence, but occasionally the thesis statement consists of two or three shorter sentences.

If the essay doesn't have too many key points, one good strategy is to preview all of the key points of the essay in the thesis statement. For example, if you are writing a business letter to apply for a job, then your thesis statement would include the main idea that you are applying for a job. It might also include the main reasons why you are qualified for the job. Here is an example:

Example Thesis Statement

I believe that I am qualified for this job for three reasons: I have experience as a chemistry lab assistant in high school, I am a chemistry major here at the college, and I am a very organized and careful worker.

Body Paragraphs

The middle of the essay is the *body*. For the topics on the CAHSEE, most essays will have two to four body paragraphs, depending on how many key points your essay contains.

In a longer essay, each paragraph in the body must relate to one of the key points of the essay, and everything in the paragraph must work together to support that point. In shorter essays, two or more points will sometimes be included in the same paragraph.

Key Points

The number of body paragraphs in your essay depends on the number of *key points* that are in the essay. Key points include the main evidence and arguments that support your essay's thesis, or main idea, and, if possible, each key point should be developed in its own paragraph.

It is a good idea to do some prewriting first to get some idea of how many key points and body paragraphs you will have before you start to write the actual essay. (For tips on prewriting techniques, see the section on *prewriting* in Chapter 8.)

To continue the example of the letter of application for the position of chemistry lab assistant, each of the three points listed in the thesis statement will have one paragraph in the body:

Body Paragraph One: Specific information about your experience as a chemistry lab assistant in high school.

Body Paragraph Two: Details about the chemistry major and the chemistry classes you have taken at the college

Body Paragraph Three: Examples that show that you are a very organized and careful worker.

Support for Key Points

Each key point needs to be supported by arguments, examples, facts, observations, and/or any other information that helps to make your point. These *supporting details*, along with the key points they support, make up each body paragraph of the essay.

In the letter of application, Body Paragraph One would include supporting details like the following: how long you were a lab assistant, including when and how long you worked as a lab assistant, what your duties were, and who your supervisor was. Body Paragraph Two would give the specific chemistry classes that you have taken or are currently taking, any related classes, how far along in the program you are (the third semester out of four semesters, for example), and types of lab experiments and demonstrations you have participated in.

Body Paragraph Three would include examples of projects that you have worked on, and maybe a few lines telling how you organized something at work or on a class project.

Transitions

Within each body paragraph there should be a clear indication of movement from one major point to the next and from one supporting detail to the next. This can be accomplished by the use of transition words that show *time order* (also called chronological order), *additional information*, *reasons or causes*, *contrasts*, or other patterns of organization.

Short Transitions

Transitions of chronological order include *first*, *next*, *then*, *after that*, *finally*, and others. Transitions of addition include *also*, *moreover*, *other* and *another*, *in addition*, *furthermore*, and similar words. Transitions of cause and effect include *because*, *for*, *as a result*, *for that reason*, *so*, *consequently*, and similar expressions. Transitions that show contrast include *but*, *yet*, *however*, *although*, *nevertheless*, and other similar words.

Longer Transitions

In addition to these shorter transitions, you can use a *phrase* (group of words) to show a transition. Some examples of phrases include *on the other* hand, *at the end of the evening*, *the most important reason*, and *in spite of the elaborate preparations*. Some longer transitions can even consist of complete clauses (with a subject and a verb), such as "Although the main character was unaware of the events that had happened..." or "When the music ended and the lights dimmed at the end of the evening...."

Try to include one or more longer transitions in your essay and to use enough other transitions to help the reader follow the organization of the essay. However, avoid adding transitions for every detail or minor point in the essay.

Transitions Between Paragraphs

When you start a new body paragraph on a new topic, you should be sure that there is a smooth shift from the previous paragraph. It is often easiest to refer back to the previous paragraph in the first sentence of the new paragraph, but you should also consider placing the transition sentence at the end of the previous paragraph.

A transition between the first two body paragraphs in the job application business letter might read something like the following:

In addition to my experience as a chemistry lab assistant, my college chemistry classes, including lab experiments, have given me more in-depth knowledge of chemistry as well as further practice in chemistry lab situations.

This sentence could be the last sentence of the first body paragraph or the topic sentence of the second body paragraph, whichever seems to work best.

Interesting Details and Specific Language

Specific details are always more interesting than general details. For example, if the purpose of your essay is to convince someone to eat more nutritional food and less junk food, you should include specific examples of what kinds of foods are important to eat.

The following sentence is very general:

It is important to eat a variety of fruits and vegetables.

A better sentence would specify some important details:

It is important to eat a variety of fruits and vegetables, such as citrus fruits or tomatoes for vitamin C and green leafy vegetables such as romaine lettuce, spinach, and Swiss chard for vitamins A and E.

It is also important to use specific words rather than general ones. For example, if you write, *We had a perfect sunny day for collecting shells at the beach*, the reader will have a much better idea of what you want to communicate than if you just wrote, *We had a good day.*

As you write practice essays and as you are writing your essay for the CAHSEE, try to include enough interesting details and specific language so that your readers will understand what you want to communicate.

The Conclusion

A conclusion can be one sentence or a whole paragraph, and will be different for each type of essay. In general, the conclusion should let the reader know that the essay is finished. Any of the following techniques can accomplish this goal:

- Reemphasize the main points and especially the thesis of the essay

- State a logical conclusion about the topic

- Emphasize the importance of the topic

- Look to the future.

There are also other ways to end an essay or business letter. In general, anything that makes the essay feel finished and complete can make an effective conclusion.

An effective conclusion for the job application business letter might read something like the following:

I believe that my experience, education, and organizational skills qualify me for this position, and that you will be pleased with my job performance. I hope to hear back from you in the near future.

Unity and Clarity

All of the parts of the essay, including the introduction, the body, and the conclusion, need to work together to clearly support the *thesis*, or *main idea*, of the essay. When all of the parts of the essay work together, the essay has *unity*.

Always stick to the *main idea* of your essay. For example, if your essay topic is about the *personality* of a character in one of the readings, you will probably not include much information about the *setting* or the *action* of the story except when it provides information that helps to analyze that character's personality.

Also, in the job application business letter, you probably would not include information about classes that are not related to the job duties, your personal hobbies or free time activities, or information about your family. In general, remember this advice: **Stick to the point**.

Types of Essays

For the final part of the CAHSEE test, you will be asked to write one essay that is randomly chosen from six different essay types. (*Note:* The State Department of Education CAHSEE materials list only five types because they group *analytical essays* and *informational essays* together as *expository writing*. However, there are some important differences between them, so this book covers them separately.)

The six essay types are as follows:

- Response to Literature

- Analytical Essay (Expository Writing)

- Informational Essay (Expository Writing)

- Persuasive Composition

- Biographical Narrative

- Business Letter

This chapter provides general tips and sample questions for each of these types of writing, along with some actual essay questions from previous CAHSEE tests (used by permission). A scoring guide and sample student essays are also provided.

For more information on each type of essay assignment, read the section called "Writing Applications Strand" in the State Department of Education *English-Language Arts Student Guide* (available online at http://www.cde.ca.gov/ta/tg/hs/elaguide.asp.)

Response to Literature

A *response to literature* essay means exactly what it says—you must read a very short story or other piece of literature and then answer some questions about it by writing an essay. (For more information on analyzing readings, see Chapter 3.)

General Tips

Show that You Understand the Reading Selection

It is important to show that you understand the reading selection. One good strategy is to begin the essay with a summary of the story. For example, *In this story, two young men discover that being a true friend requires more effort than just hanging around together* or, *In this story, Ethan wrestles with mixed emotions when his best friend beats him in the orchestra competition.* (For more information on summarizing, see Chapter 4.)

Thesis Statement

Remember that a good thesis statement always lets the reader know what the main idea of your essay is. A good place for the thesis statement is right after the summary of the reading. Make this statement clear and direct, and be sure that it matches the assigned topic.

Support Your Points

Make sure that your thesis and any other points you make are supported by quotes from the reading. (For more information on quotations, see Chapter 7).

Possible Response to Literature Essay Topics

A response to literature essay assignment will probably include two or more questions similar to the ones that follow:

Character Analysis

- Describe the personality, emotions, and/or motivation of _____ (a specified character or characters in the story).

- Discuss how _____ (a specified character)'s emotions and personality affect the action of the story.

- How does the author reveal _____ (a character)'s emotions (or personality or motivation)?

Character Interactions

- Describe the relationship between two specified characters (or groups of characters).

- Describe how the relationship between two specified characters (or groups of characters) affects the events of the story.

- How does the author reveal the relationship between two specified characters (or groups of characters)?

Literary Devices

- How does the author use setting (or dialogue, or other literary devices) in the story?

- How does the author organize the story? How does the organization of the story contribute to its effectiveness?

You will also be given a standard checklist to follow while writing your response, which you will find with each of the actual CAHSEE essay questions in this chapter.

Analytical Essay

An *analytical essay* is a response to a nonfiction article or essay. In this type of writing assignment, you are asked to read a selection and then write an essay on an assigned topic, with supporting details and evidence taken from the reading.

An analytical essay is similar to a *response to literature essay* in that both types of essay require you to write a response to something that you have read.

General Tips

Show that You Understand the Reading Selection

It is important to show that you understand the reading selection. One way to do this is to write a short summary of the reading selection at the very beginning of your essay.

Thesis Statement

A good thesis statement will help you keep your essay on track. Make sure that your thesis statement is clear and direct and that it matches the topic you have been assigned to write on.

Support Your Points

Make sure that your thesis and any other points you make are supported by quotes from the reading. (For more information on using quotations, see Chapter 7).

Actual CAHSEE Analytical Essay Topic

The following essay and writing assignment appeared on a previous administration of the CAHSEE. (Used by permission.)

The following article offers information on hummingbirds. Read the article and write your response to the writing prompt that follows.

Hummingbirds

A flicker of color off to the side catches my eye as I walk along the back fence. It is a warm May morning, and I am outside early to see how the lettuce I've planted is doing. The wire mesh fence that edges my back yard is draped in blue and white morning glories just starting to open in the morning sun. The flicker of color off to my left becomes more pronounced, and I turn, expecting to see a butterfly hovering over the flowers. Instead, a tiny green bird with a red throat is hanging upside down above one of the morning glory blossoms. It is bigger than the butterfly and has a long bill protruding from its tiny head. The bird I have sighted above the morning glories is a male ruby-throated hummingbird, the most common species in the eastern United States.

The hummingbird is found only in the Western Hemisphere and belongs to the *Trochilidae* family, which contains more than 300 species of "hummers," as they are known among enthusiasts. Sporting an emerald green back with gray flanks and an iridescent ruby-red throat, this bird is also called *Joyas Voladoras* or "flying jewels" in Spanish because of its brilliant colors.

With an average length of 3.5 inches and weighing only one eighth of an ounce, this hummingbird is incredibly quick, flying at speeds of 30 miles per hour and diving at speeds of up to 65 miles per hour. Hummingbirds' brains make up almost 2.5 percent of their overall weight, making them proportionately, the largest-brained in the bird kingdom, yet the flying muscles comprise some 30 percent of the bird's tiny weight. With these flying muscles, hummingbirds have the fastest wing rate of any bird, which helps them on their migratory paths that can cover up to 2,000 miles between Canada and Panama.

Hummingbirds use their speed to be aggressive feeders and become very territorial. They will fiercely fight one another for sources of food, diving and colliding in midair, and using their bills and claws as weapons. The tremendous speeds at which hummingbirds fly require that they feed constantly. One bird may visit a thousand flowers a day in search of food, munching on gnats, spiders, and sapsuckers, feeding every 10 minutes, and eating almost two thirds of its body weight every day. Like butterflies, they also feed on the pollen and nectar of flowers, sucking out this drink through a long tube-like tongue that absorbs the liquid through capillary action.

The most remarkable aspect of the hummingbirds' wing function is that the wings can rotate fully, making them the only birds that can fly forward, backward, up, down, sideways, or simply hover in space. This ability makes the tiny birds seem like magical creatures. They can hang poised over a blossom, or they can appear to stand still in midair. When hovering in this apparent stationary position, they are actually moving their wings in a figure eight pattern, and from this position can move in any direction.

On this particular morning, I continue my stroll along the perimeter of the fence. I see two more hummingbirds: one a female who lacks the ruby iridescence at its throat, but who sports a white breast; the other, a male with the ruby gorget. Since it is spring, I wonder if the female is nesting or if her two eggs have hatched. I hope that each season brings more of the tiny, brilliant birds to my backyard, where I can enjoy their aerodynamic antics and their brilliant flashes of color.

Writing Task:

In this essay about hummingbirds, the author describes many of the bird's characteristics. In each paragraph, she supports the purpose of her essay. What is the author's purpose for writing this essay about hummingbirds? What details does she give to support her purpose?

Write an essay in which you discuss the author's purpose for writing this essay on hummingbirds. What details and examples does she use to support the purpose of her essay?

Checklist for Your Writing

The following checklist will help you do your best work. Make sure you:

- ❏ Read the selection and the description of the task carefully.

- ❏ Use specific details and examples from the reading selection to demonstrate your understanding of the selection's main ideas and the author's purpose.

- ❏ Organize your writing with a strong introduction, body, and conclusion.

- ❏ Choose specific words that are appropriate for your audience and purpose.

- ❏ Vary your sentences to make your writing interesting to read.

- ❏ Use an appropriate tone and voice.

- ❏ Check for mistakes in grammar, spelling, punctuation, and sentence formation.

Scoring Guide and Sample Student Essays

On the following pages, you will find Sample Student Essays* and the scores given for each essay, along with commentary on why the scores were given. For more information, see the "Scoring Guide for Response to Literary/Expository Text" in the Appendix.

* Sample Student Essays are reprinted by permission from California High School Exit Exam (CAHSEE), California Department of Education, P.O. Box 271, Sacramento, CA 95812-0271.

"Analytical Essay" — *Hummingbirds*

4   **Score Point 4**
     Student Response *

                                             Commentary

The author of the story on hummingbirds likes hummingbirds for many reasons. The author enjoys the anatomy of the hummingbird. She enjoys the eating habits of hummingbirds. Another basis for her affection for the small birds is their attractive and graceful colors. She loves hummingbirds for many various reasons.

The anatomy of the hummingbird is easily enjoyed by the author. She is amazed by the fact that the hummingbird is the largest brained in the bird kingdom. She is surprised that the small bird can fly at speeds of 30 mph and five at speeds of 60 mpg. She also thinks that the hummingbird's ability to rotate it's wings in any direction is a remarkable feat. It is anatomy of the hummingbird is astonishing.

Another concept that the author finds riveting is the eating habits of the hummingbird. She is amazed by the bird's ability to shoot out its tongue and soak up nectar using a capillary action. She finds it amazing that the bird eats a diet of insects and spiders every 10 minutes.

She is also astonished by the fact that hummingbirds can eat up to 30% of their own bodyweight. It is easy to see why she is amazed of the eating habits of hummingbirds.

    Throughout this 4 response to "Hummingbirds," the writer demonstrates a thorough and thoughtful comprehensive grasp of the text through the many examples of how the author shares the way she "likes hummingbirds..." In the introduction, the writer infers through the thesis that the author is sharing her "affection for the small birds..." and that... "She loves hummingbirds for many various reasons."

    As the essay progresses, the writer develops several of the reasons the author uses to illustrate her fascination with the bird.

    In the first paragraph, the writer provides textual support to illustrate why the bird's anatomy is "enjoyed" by the author. The facts presented about the bird's brain, how fast the bird can fly, and its ability to rotate its wings are all presented to support the thesis.

    Through the discussion of the bird's anatomy, the writer draws conclusions about the ambiguities and nuances of the text with the statement that the "...anatomy of the hummingbird is astonishing."

    In the third paragraph, the writer provides more textual support with a discussion about the bird's eating habits. The writer mentions that the author finds the bird's eating habits "riveting." More discussion on the bird's eating habits is done in the fourth paragraph.

---

* The student response has been typed as written, with the student's own content, grammar, spelling, and punctuation.

Probably the thing she loves the most about the hummingbird is it's beauty. She loves the ruby red color of it's neck. She is lured into loving them by the females majestic, white chest. She is captured by their emerald colored back. It is no wonder why the author adores such a beautiful creature.

I think almost anyone can relate to the author's love towards hummingbirds. With their amazing anatomy and extraordinary eating habits it is easy to be amazed by them. Plus, their amazing grace and beauty is enough to keep anyone satisfied. It is no wonder why the author loves the majestic hummingbird.

The writer decides that the author probably loves the hummingbird's beauty the most. This idea is NOT explicitly stated in the text; the writer determined this importance through the thoughtful choice of textual details and support from the text.

In the final paragraph, the conclusion is drawn that "…almost anyone can relate to the author's love towards hummingbirds." It is through this conclusion that the writer connects to the readers' expectations and potential misunderstandings.

Throughout the writer's entire essay, the only errors one finds are first-draft in nature. The writer provides a variety of sentence types and uses descriptive language within many of the sentences to enhance the readers' understanding of how fascinated the author of the text is with hummingbirds.

This is a clear example of a 4 response to literature.

3   **Score Point 3**
     Student Response *
                                                Commentary

I feel that the authors purpose for writing <u>Hummingbirds</u> was to Facinate you and get you interested about hummingbirds.

The author does this many ways. She talks about facts that probably first interested her. She says in the third paragraph, for example, that Humming girds brains make up almost 2.5% of the birds over all weight. Now, this did get me some what interested and it did support her purpose. It also sounded like it was something she was interested in as well wich I thought was kind of neat. She also wrote about Humming birds wings kind of captured my attenion and did what I think it was ment to do facinate me.

I also think that the author was trying to paint a picture In our head of the animals in action. For example she explains how "they can hang poised over a blossom, or they can appear to stand still in mid air." I think she was trying to paint a picture of a "magical creature" in our minds therefore facinating us farther.

Overall the author facinated me more than any other author had with the rest of the stories. I believe that was the purpose and it worked.

In this 3 response, the writer provides a thesis in the first, one-sentence paragraph suggesting that the author's purpose "...was to Facinate you and get you interested about hummingbirds."

The writer provides textual support illustrating a comprehensive grasp of the text and supporting the idea that the author's purpose "...was to Facinate you and get you interested about hummingbirds."

A general understanding of the nuances of the text is evident as the writer provides facts about the bird's brains, wings, and how the bird "...can hang poised over a blossom..." As the facts are presented, the writer shares how he/she became fascinated by the facts the author presented. ("...wich I thought was kind of neat," "...kind of captured my attention...")

The writer concludes with the idea that the author "...fascinated me more than any other author had..." which was "...the purpose and it worked."

Overall, the writer provides a thesis and general support illustrating a general understanding of the text.

There is an existence of sentence variety and descriptive language. There are some errors in the conventions of the English language, but they do not interfere with the readers' understanding of the essay. ("...*Facinates, interested, birds* (bird's), *wich*, etc.)

This is a clear example of a 3 response to the literature.

---

* The student response has been typed as written, with the student's own content, grammar, spelling, and punctuation.

2   **Score Point 2**
     Student Response *

Commentary

the authors purpose for writing this essay is her facination with humming birds. She give many details to support her topics. In her essay the author describes hummingbirds vivdy. She states some different kinds of hummingbirds, like, <u>trochilidae</u>, there are more than 300 types of hummingbirds in that group of birds. The author also states the many different types of birds and the colors they might be. She also gives examples of a bird she saw in her back yard, she also told a story about them.

In this 2 response, the writer provides a limited thesis within the statement that "the authors purpose for writing this essay is her facination with humming birds." The writer states that the author "…describes hummingbirds vivdy," but fails to provide any of the specifics provided by the author of the text. The writer only mentions that these facts exist, but with the exception of the fact that "Trochilidae" are a type of hummingbird, the writer does no more than to mention the idea that the author gave examples and told a story about them (the birds).

Through this essay, the writer provides no more than a limited comprehensive grasp of the text. The few details provided support the main idea but lack any details. At the sentence level, there is no evidence of much variety in sentence types and there are several errors in the conventions of the English language. (*the* should be The, *facination, vividy*, etc.) There is also a lack of evidence of much control at the sentence level.

This 2 essay is an example of a limited response to the prompt.

* The student response has been typed as written, with the student's own content, grammar, spelling, and punctuation.

1

Score Point 1
Student Response *

Commentary

The lady wrote the essay about hummingbirds because she really likes them. She's trying to show other people how amazing this little creatures really are.

In this 1 response, the writer only responds to one, simple idea that "the lady," whom the reader assumes is the author, "...really likes them." (The reader also assumes that "them" refers to hummingbirds.) The simple statement that "she's trying to show other people how amazing this little creatures really are," is all that is provided. There is NO attempt to provide textual details or support. There is no sentence variety since there are no more than two sentences in the entire essay. There is little evidence of serious errors in the conventions of the English language, but the errors in the second sentence suggest a lack of control of convention. Overall, there is not enough provided by the writer to score this essay higher than a 1.

* The student response has been typed as written, with the student's own content, grammar, spelling, and punctuation.

Informational Essay

An informational essay informs the reader about something. To get the highest possible score on this type of essay, be sure to include a thesis statement that includes the main point of the essay, as well as specific supporting details that include facts and details.

General Tips

Anticipating Questions or Objections

No matter what topic you write on, not all of your readers will accept or agree with the information you are telling them in the essay. One good strategy for dealing with this kind of possible bias is to ask yourself what objections your readers may have, and try to answer those objections in your essay.

For example, on an essay about study tips, you might include the importance of getting a good night's sleep. If you anticipate that some readers may think that this information is not important or not true, you should support this point in your essay. One way to do this would be by providing more information about how getting enough sleep helps students get higher grades on tests and helps them pay more attention in class.

Example Informational Essay Assignments

If you are assigned an informational essay, it will be on a topic that should be familiar to you, such as the following two sample assignments:

Example 1.

You have taken quite a few classes in high school. Think about one of the classes you have taken. What information would help a new student do well in that class?

Write an essay describing one of your classes in high school to a new student. Include any tips for doing well in the class. Use details and examples to illustrate your points.

Example 2.

Choose one place at your school where you feel comfortable or happy. Write an essay describing that place, and explain why that place makes you feel that way. Include details and examples to support your points.

Persuasive Composition

Persuasive writing is writing that tries to convince the reader of something. In order to be effective, a persuasive essay must be organized very clearly and logically, and include clear arguments with good supporting details.

General Tips

Organization of a Persuasive Essay

Make your main point first (the point that you are trying to convince your readers of) and support it with at least two reasons (three or four if possible) and other types of evidence in the body of the paper. Develop each of the reasons with facts and details.

Be sure that you also anticipate your readers' objections and address them in the body of the paper. To do this, imagine that you are in a debate. Ask yourself what arguments your opponent might make against your main point and include them in your paper. When you include an objection, also show why your point is stronger than your opponent's objection.

The next step is to finish with a good, clear conclusion. It's a good idea to restate your main point again.

Various Types of Appeals

There are several ways to try to persuade (or *appeal* to) your readers. The first way is to use *logic* by making reasonable statements that the reader can understand and agree with. This is called an *appeal to reason*.

Another way to appeal to your readers is to *appeal to the readers' emotions or ethical beliefs*. You can also use real life *examples* from your personal experience or someone you know. Finally, comparisons with real situations (*analogies*) can often be used to effectively support a thesis.

Actual CAHSEE Persuasive Essay Topic

The following writing assignment appeared on a previous administration of the CAHSEE. (Used by permission.)

Writing Task:

> Some students at your school have expressed an interest in making the school more attractive by getting rid of the trash on the school grounds.
>
> Write a persuasive essay for your school paper in which you convince the readers of the importance of getting rid of the trash and making the school more attractive. Convince your readers through the use of specific reasons and examples.
>
> **Checklist for Your Writing**
>
> The following checklist will help you do your best work. Make sure you:
>
> ❑ Read the description of the task carefully.
>
> ❑ Organize your writing with a strong introduction, body, and conclusion.
>
> ❑ State your position, support it with specific examples, and address the reader's concerns.
>
> ❑ Use words that are appropriate for your audience and purpose.
>
> ❑ Vary your sentences to make your writing interesting to read.
>
> ❑ Check for mistakes in grammar, spelling, punctuation, capitalization, and sentence formation.

Scoring Guide and Sample Student Essays

On the following pages, you will find Sample Student Essays* and the scores given for each essay, along with commentary on why the scores were given. For more information about scoring essays, see the "Scoring Guide for Response to Writing Prompt" in the Appendix.

* Sample Student Essays are reprinted by permission from California High School Exit Exam (CAHSEE), California Department of Education, P.O. Box 271, Sacramento, CA 95812-0271.

"Response to Writing Prompt"—Persuasive Composition

4 **Score Point 4**
Student Response *

Commentary

Would you enjoy taking your classes at the city dump? Trash is not beautiful. It is a well-known fact that students learn better when they're in a clean environment. To be more attractive, trash on our school grounds must be picked up. The importance of picking up trash is to beautify our campus and make our school a healthier place to learn.

We want our campus to be attractive and clean, right? When rival schools come to compete against us, we don't want them going home criticizing us because of our campus. We don't want our mascot become a rat or a pig in their eyes. We want to keep our campus clean to show that we're not slobs and are educated enough to pick up our own garbage.

Who would want to eat lunch inside a dumpster? Or exercise in a gym that smells like rotten eggs and spoiled milk? We need a campus that will make it easier and healthier to learn. Would essays show the student's best if they brainstormed ideas while looking out the window at old food, used bandaids, empty soda cans and gum wrappers? The way this campus looks influenses the way we perform in our classrooms. To get the

In this response, the writer addresses all parts of the persuasive writing task: stating a position about the importance of cleaning up trash, defending the position with evidence, and anticipating the reader's concerns. The first paragraph gives the writer's position ("trash on our school grounds must be picked up") and then gives two reasons that picking up trash is very important ("to beautify our campus and make our school a healthier place to learn"). These two ideas become the focus for the rest of the essay.

The writer uses the questions that open each of the next two paragraphs to anticipate objections to cleaning up trash, thereby addressing the reader's potential concerns. The second paragraph provides several images to support the argument that a more attractive campus would provide specific benefits (e.g., "We don't want our mascot to become a rat or a pig in their [rival schools'] eyes"). Although the third paragraph provides little detail about the health aspects of the argument, it does use specific details to develop the concept that a clean environment is conducive to learning. The essay provides a strong conclusion that not only restates the writer's position but also extends the argument with a call to

---

* The student response has been typed as written, with the student's own content, grammar, spelling, and punctuation.

maximum quality work done, we need clean and sanitary workspaces.

In conclusion, picking up any trash around school will be beneficial to everybody, especially us. If you see a piece of paper blowin around stop it with your foot and bend down, pick it up, then throw it away. There's no reason why our campus needs to be anything other than attractive. With everyone's help, it can be attractive and provide a better learning atmosphere.

action: "If you see a piece of paper blowin around, stop it with your foot and bend down, pick it up, then throw it away".

The essay demonstrates the control of organization that is required for a 4-point paper, and the stated position is developed with details. Although there is a misplaced modifier ("To be more attractive, trash..."), and a few additional errors in conventions, overall the writer demonstrates control of conventions. The essay also uses a variety of sentence types and precise, descriptive language. Overall, this essay is a sample of a 4-point response.

3 **Score Point 3**
Student Response *

Commentary

Nobody would like it if people stopped picking up trash and let our school become filled with trash. It is very important to keep our school clean to provide an appropriate learning environment. If everyone would help out our school would look more attractive.

A clean school campus would offer a nicer and appropriate learning environment. A dirty school makes it harder to concentrate on school work. If trash covered the campus students might be looking out classroom windows for what awaits them after class and wondering why someone is not cleaning it up. A clean school would help the students concentrate so grades might raise not only making the school look better on the outside but academically as well.

No one enjoys being in a dirty environment. Before school, snack, lunch, and after school would be much less enjoyable to both the students and faculty if our campus was dirty. People do not like eating in trash filled lunch areas and so there would be more students leaving school permitted or not for lunch. Basically, students and teachers would not be able to stand being in a dirty environment during school hours.

In conclusion living environments are kept clean and so it is equally important to keep learning environments clean as well. Both the students and faculty spend large portions of their days here so to make school a little better and more attractive our school needs to be kept clean. It would be easy if everyone just did their part.

In this response to the writing prompt, the writer begins with a paragraph that states three positions about picking up trash—that "Nobody would like" a school "filled with trash," that a clean school provides "an appropriate learning environment," and that a clean school would "look more attractive." The paragraphs that follow discuss each of these ideas.

The second paragraph of the essay focuses on the learning environment, explaining that students can concentrate better if there is no trash on campus. The third paragraph addresses the idea that "no one enjoys being in a dirty environment." The final paragraph restates the idea that the school could look more attractive if everyone helped.

In general, the paper defends the three positions with some details and examples, but the development is not as thoughtful or thorough as that in a 4-point paper. In the third paragraph, for example, each sentence restates the topic sentence and adds only a few additional details.

The paper addresses readers' concerns and expectations in a general way by stating that "Nobody would like it if people stopped picking up trash" and "No one enjoys being in a dirty environment," and thus a general sense of audience is evident throughout the essay.

There are a few errors in the conventions of written English, but they do not interfere with the reader's understanding. Overall, this essay is an example of a 3-point response to this writing task.

* The student response has been typed as written, with the student's own content, grammar, spelling, and punctuation.

2 **Score Point 2**   **Commentary**
   Student Response *

The importance of getting rid of garbage on school camps is very important. The importance of getting rid of the garbage is makeing are school look nice, giving less work for the teachers and janitors to do. Another reason it is important because if I don't look oke people are going to think that it isn't a good school.

I think that this a good subject to write on because the trash on school campus is terrible. School campuses have alot of garbage because people don't care about throwing there trash away. But people need to think more reasonsivly because they are destroying the earth if they do not pick up there garbage. So people from now on when you have garbage don't throw it on the ground throw it in the garbage can.

Another reason it is important for people not to litter because this where we live and we don't need to destroy where we live. Pluse what would other people come to our school meaning the district office people think of us if we just left our trash all over the ground that would make us look bad.

In this response to the writing prompt, the writer begins by stating three reasons that picking up trash is important: "makeing are school look nice," "giving less work for the teachers and janitors to do," and preventing people from thinking "that it isn't a good school."

Although the paper states these positions with some authority, it fails to support them in the paragraphs that follow. The second paragraph focuses on a new, although related, topic, that people should pick up their trash to avoid destroying the earth. The third paragraph moves from the idea that trash destroys the earth to the idea that it destroys "where we live." This paragraph also contains an attempt to develop the third position in the opening paragraph, that having trash around suggests that this isn't a good school: "if we just left our trash all over the ground that would make us look bad."

This essay provides little or no support for its thesis, shows little control over organization, and demonstrates an inconsistent tone and focus. It also fails to anticipate readers' concerns. These factors, in addition to the lack of control over the conventions of written English, particularly spelling, make this essay an example of a 2-point response.

* The student response has been typed as written, with the student's own content, grammar, spelling, and punctuation.

1   **Score Point 1**
     Student Response *

Commentary

It would be a good idea to clean up our enviremet, maybe if there was more trash cans well you could make our schlool cleaner if just everybody picked up on thing our schlool would not be 3/4ths clean that's how bad our mess has gotten to who wants to attend a school that's now for the trash and ants and roaches etc. No one does that's why we should clean our school & our great reward in the end a clean & safe and healthy enviremet and school.

In this response to the writing prompt, the writer begins with the position that cleaning up the environment is a good idea. This statement is followed by two suggestions—that there could be more trash cans and that everyone should help pick up trash. Another topic follows, which is a description of the extent of the trash problem at school, and then the final sentence of the response reaffirms that cleaning up trash will have beneficial results.

This response offers several ideas related to the topic but fails to support these ideas with details or examples. In addition, the response lacks consistency of focus and fails to demonstrate a control of organization. The serious errors in the conventions of written English, particularly in sentence boundaries, interfere with the reader's understanding of the essay and result in a score of 1.

* The student response has been typed as written, with the student's own content, grammar, spelling, and punctuation.

Biographical Narrative

The CAHSEE exam may ask you to write a *biographical narrative* (from the root words *bio = life*, and *graph = writing*). A *biographical narrative* is an essay that tells a story about a person's life.

General Tips

Choosing the Right Person to Write About

If you are assigned one of these topics, choose a person that you are very familiar with or that you know a lot about. If possible, choose someone that you feel close to or that you respect and admire.

Preparing to Write

After you have chosen a person to write about, use a prewriting technique to get some information down on paper. (For a review of prewriting techniques, see Chapter 8.)

Listing

One technique that may work well for this type of essay is *listing*. To make a list for a biographical narrative, draw a line down the center of a piece of scratch paper. On one side of the line, write some words that describe the person's personality or how he or she is with other people. These words might be adjectives like *stern*, *fair*, *protective*, *caring*, *fun-loving*, *dependable*, or any other words that describe the person.

The next step is to think about some experiences this person had that show how that person is. For example, if you wrote *loyal* on one side of the line, on the other side you might write

The time she (or he) came to my birthday party even though she had an invitation to see the Lakers

and/or

The time she (or he) took the blame for knocking over the lamp when we were both wrestling on the floor

If you wrote more than one adjective, list examples for several of them. Then pick at least one characteristic to write about. If you think the story will be very short, you might want to include more than one story about the same person.

Introduction and Thesis Statement

The next step is to start writing about the person you chose. In your introduction and thesis statement, be sure to identify the person and to include the main point of the story. For example, if the story shows how loyal that person is, you should mention that in the thesis statement. Here is an example:

My friend Anna is a very loyal person who has kept me from getting into trouble on several occasions.

Organizing The Details

For most biographical essays, you will probably want to tell everything that happened in chronological order: the order in which it happened (first things first). Then finish up with a good strong conclusion.

Specific Details

Try to include specific details including where and when the action took place and sensory details including colors, sounds, and maybe smells; temperature, texture and other touch sensations; or tastes.

Example Biographical Essay Assignments

If you are assigned a biographical essay, you will be asked to write about a person you know a lot about, as in the following two sample assignments:

Example 1.

> Write about a person you know personally that you admire or who has helped you. Explain why this person has a special place in your life. Include details and examples to illustrate your points.

Example 2.

> Write about a superstar in music, art, sports, or science who is alive today. Explain what makes this person different from most people. Use details and examples to support your points.

Business Letter

Types and Purposes of Business Letters

Strictly speaking, a business letter is not an essay, but it is one of the types of writing that might be assigned on the CAHSEE test. Business letters are different from personal letters because they are usually written to people that you don't know very well personally.

General Tips

Content

Some examples of business letters include letters to recommend somebody for a job or to apply for a job yourself, letters of complaint about poor quality merchandise or service, proposals to provide a service or merchandise, and other similar topics. A business letter can contain persuasive writing, informational (expository) writing, biographical writing, or a combination of any of these.

(For more information about types of writing, refer to the first part of this chapter. To review the steps of the writing process and other useful information, refer to Chapters 8 and 9.)

Consider Your Reader

Adapt your writing style depending on who your reader is and the purpose of your paper. If you are writing a letter of complaint, for example, be polite but firm, and be very specific about what you are asking for (your money back, other compensation, an apology, a promise to do better in the future, etc.).

Probably the most important strategy for business letters is to make them direct, clear, and very specific. The easier they are to read and understand, the better chance they have of getting you the results you want.

Format

Business letters should be word-processed or typed whenever possible, usually in a traditional font, but the CAHSEE might ask you to write one by hand. The important thing is to write or print as clearly and as neatly as possible.

Business letters include the *date* and the *recipient's address* at the top, then a *salutation* such as Dear _____. After that is the *body* of the letter, and then a *closing* such as "Sincerely," the *sender's signature*, and the *sender's address and contact information*, usually at the end. Sometimes the sender's information is included at the top, especially if you are writing on letterhead paper that is already printed with your name, address, and contact information.

There are several formats for business letters, but they all follow the same basic organization and design. You can use any business letter format that you are familiar with. If you do not have a favorite format, the block method is easy to learn and very clear to read. In the block method, each part of the letter is lined up on the left edge of the paper, as in the example below:

Illustration of Block Method

Date

Recipient's Name and Title
Street Address
City, State Zip

Dear _____ ,

The block format is very easy to read and type because everything starts on the left side. The typist does not have to set any tabs, so this method is also an efficient one. Another important point is that it is easy to remember.

Whichever format you use, use a "Return" between paragraphs. This keeps the major ideas separate from each other and also looks nice on the page. Where academic papers are almost always indented, business letters in block style are not.

This section of this book will help prepare you in case you are asked to write a business letter on the CAHSEE exam. Good luck on your upcoming test and writing assignment.

Sincerely,

(Sign your name here)

Your Name (printed or typed)
Your Street Address
Your City, State Zip
Your Email and/or
Phone and/or
Fax Number (optional)

Example Business Letter Assignments

At the date of publication of this book, no sample business letter writing assignments had been released by the California State Department of Education. However, the questions might be similar to the following:

- Write a business letter to your high school principal requesting him or her to form a new club on campus. If possible, pick a club that you would be interested in participating in. (If you don't know the principal's name, use Ms. Smith or Mr. Jones.)

- Write a business letter to the U.S. Postal Service to complain about receiving too much junk mail and asking what you can do to reduce the amount you receive.

CAHSEE
English-Language Arts

Practice Test 1

Practice Test

1

The following article discusses the sport of falconry. Read the article and answer questions 1 through 5.

On Becoming a Falconer*

Falconry, an ancient sport popular in the days of medieval royalty and jousting tournaments, is still practiced by dedicated enthusiasts around the world. Falconers work with predatory birds ranging from expert fliers, like the peregrine falcon, to less spectacular hawks, such as the redtail. Regardless of the species, training is the most important part of falconry. But it can be frustrating; so, you must be very patient.

The first step in training your falcon is to establish her trust in you. Initially, the falcon won't allow you near—she will "bate," or beat her wings wildly, as you approach. But gradually you will coax her to fly to you by offering food. The proud and cautious bird will be reluctant to fly

---

Note: Readings marked with an asterisk (*) are reprinted, by permission, from *California High School Exit Exam (CAHSEE)*, California Department of Education, P.O. Box 271, Sacramento, CA 95812-0271.

to your hand, but she will want the food there and she will move back and forth on her perch, stamping her feet. Suddenly she will leave her perch. She may land on your hand and bate off right away, frightened by her own bravery at first. Sooner or later, however, she will return to feed, and that will be her first careful step toward accepting you.

Why do falconers love this sport? To understand falconry, you must understand the special nature of the bond that forms between the falconer and the bird. The wild behavior and skills of the falcon are treasured by the falconer. The reward in working with a trained falcon is the companionship of a creature that can choose at any time to disappear over the horizon forever. You can join the honored tradition of falconers if you have patience and respect for wild creatures.

1. What does the phrase *disappear over the horizon* mean in the following sentence?

> The reward in working with a trained falcon is the companionship of creatures that can choose at any time to disappear over the horizon forever.

A return to the falconer

B abandon the falconer

C go behind some trees

D fly very high

2. According to the article, which of the following summarizes the main reason modern falconers love their sport?

A It allows them to work with a creature that is normally wild.

B It was popular among royalty of the Middle Ages.

C The falcon bates the falconer.

D They like the reward money from the sport.

3. Which of the following MOST accurately indicates the author's attitude toward the sport of falconry?

A It is not suited to modern times.

B It can be frustrating.

C It is best to work with a peregrine falcon.

D It is a rewarding experience.

4. The phrase "disappear over the horizon" communicates a(n) _____ image.

A optimistic

B matter-of-fact

C sarcastic

D sad

5. A wild animal that trusts people might seem _____.

A contradictory

B ambiguous

C subtle

D traditional

The following newspaper article is about electric cars. Read the newspaper article and answer questions 6 through 11.

Electric Cars Deserve a Second Look*

As the world becomes increasingly populated, it is also becoming alarmingly polluted. We deplete more resources, produce more waste, and cause more cumulative environmental strain than ever before.

Fortunately, there are many ways that you can help counter the negative effects that we impose on the environment. One of these is driving an electric car. This benefits not only the environment, but also individual drivers.

Electric cars produce about 80 percent less pollution than cars with gas-powered motors. In fact, the only reason that electric cars produce any pollution at all is that their electric energy is generated by power plants—electric cars themselves emit no exhaust. When energy comes from large sources such as power plants, it's easier to regulate and monitor, so there's less waste than if the energy is generated by many smaller sources, such as the gas engines in individual cars.

In addition, electric cars are simply more efficient than gas-powered cars for several reasons. First, electric cars have regenerative braking, which means that when you use the brakes in an electric car, the battery has a chance to recharge. Conversely, when you brake in a gas-powered car, you actually *use* energy.

Also, during the production of electric cars, more time and energy is spent making the design lighter and more aerodynamic so that there will be less drag from the wind. This allows them to travel farther using less energy than a gas-powered car would use to go the same distance.

In addition to the environmental benefits of driving electric cars, there are also financial and time-saving benefits for the drivers.

For one, they cost less to maintain. The cost of charging an electric car is about 20 percent of the cost of gas, and electric cars require far less maintenance than gas-powered cars. This is due, in part, to the fact that a lot of the things that go wrong with gas-powered cars simply aren't present in electric cars. Electric cars have no cooling system, fan belts, radiators, hoses, or oil—just a battery. There are fewer moving parts overall, so there are fewer potential problems. Also, electric motors have far greater longevity than combustion motors, so after the body of an electric car gives out, the engine can be reused in another body.

Furthermore, the federal government is encouraging electric car use by giving significant rebates for purchasing electric cars, and some states offer additional rebates.

Electric cars can also save people time. While gas-powered cars require visits to a mechanic every few months, the only routine maintenance required by electric cars is replacing the battery every four years. And California, for example, recently passed a law making it legal for drivers of electric cars to use the carpool lanes any time—even if they are driving alone. This makes your trips

much quicker and saves a considerable amount of time, especially in rush-hour traffic.

Overall, there are numerous benefits of driving an electric car. It may take a little getting used to, but in the long run, the use of electric cars can help preserve the environment and give people more time and money to be put to better use.

6. **Read this sentence from the article.**

> Furthermore, the federal government is encouraging electric car use by giving significant rebates for purchasing electric cars, and some states offer additional rebates.

What is the meaning of the word *rebates* in Darrow's article?

A money returned

B tax credits

C awards

D additional guarantees

7. **Read this sentence from the article.**

> We deplete more resources, produce more waste, and cause more cumulative environmental strain than ever before.

What does the word *deplete* in Darrow's article mean?

A   store away

B   use up

C   own

D   ruin

8. **What is the main purpose of Darrow's article?**

A   to convince readers that their cars are using too much energy

B   to show how to improve driving

C   to convince people that electric cars are good

D   to show how the environment can be saved

9. **The first paragraph of this article does which of the following?**

A   presents the main idea of the article

B   provides details that support the main idea

C   summarizes the article

D   gets the reader's attention

10. **What does the word *conversely* mean in the following sentence from this article?**

> Conversely, when you brake in a gas-powered car, you actually *use* energy.

A   furthermore

B   on the other hand

C   for example

D   consequently

11. **Read the following sentence from the article.**

> Also, electric motors have far greater longevity than combustion motors, so after the body of an electric car gives out, the engine can be reused in another body.

What does the expression *gives out* mean in this sentence?

A   goes out

B   leaves out

C   wears out

D   tries out

The following article describes some of the many positive features of the state of California. Read the article and answer questions 12 through 16.

California: A Tribute*

You do not have to travel to many other states to realize that California is a world unto itself. This is so widely recognized throughout the world that the state may as well be its own country. The Golden State is complete in itself, with a landscape ranging from desert to mountain to meadow to coastline. Snow-capped mountains rise up majestically before the ocean and golden deserts stretch over vast plains. Fragrant, fruit-scented breezes waft through valleys full of orange groves, apple orchards and vineyards. Pacific Coast Highway, also known as Highway 1, charts a sometimes winding course, edging the rugged, sea-worn cliffs, curving through the mountains, and sailing by smooth beaches, past the white-capped waves of wild surf and the glassy blue waters of the bays. Pastoral scenes of cows grazing in pastures contrast with urban views of skyscrapers and city lights.

California's population is as diverse as its geography, including people from every race and ethnic background. This diversity intensifies the beauty of the state. Music, art, and dance from every country is widely performed in towns and cities throughout the state. Dragons lead parades for the Chinese and Vietnamese New Year celebrations, the music of guitars enlivens Cinco de Mayo festivals, and drumbeats quicken the heartbeat at Brazilian Samba and African dance performances in the parks. Music from summer jazz festivals drifts over the communities while symphonies tune up for Bach festivals in the winter. All of these traditions and arts weave together to create an atmosphere of incredible intercultural beauty and richness.

The state's wealth is only increased by its eccentricities and its magic. In a small town north of San Francisco, there is a ranch populated with horses no bigger than large dogs. In the coastal city of Santa Cruz, a favorite tourist attraction is the Mystery Spot, a place where the rules of gravity don't seem to apply and objects actually roll uphill. The Monterey Bay region hosts hordes of regal black and orange Monarch butterflies during their annual migration. Swallows return yearly to San Juan

Capistrano, perhaps because, like anyone who has traveled to California, they cannot bear to leave the Golden State forever.

12. What does the word *eccentricities* mean in the following sentence?

> The state's wealth is only increased by its eccentricities and its magic.

A   unusual characteristics

B   large population

C   diverse climate

D   famous beauty

13. Which of the following lines from the article BEST supports its theme?

A   "Fragrant, fruit-scented breezes waft through valleys full of orange groves."

B   "The state's wealth is only increased by its eccentricities and its magic."

C   "You don't have to travel to many other states to realize that California is a world unto itself."

D   "California's population is as diverse as its geography."

14. Which of the following strategies does the author use MOST frequently to describe California?

A   imagery

B   statistics

C   expert opinion

D   historical fact

15. The author's use of descriptive language gives this article a(n) _____ tone?

A   neutral

B   questioning

C   judgmental

D   enthusiastic

16. What does the author believe about California?

A   It is a humorous place.

B   It is a wonderful place.

C   It is an ordinary place.

D   It is a melancholy place.

The following is a story about two friends on a journey through the woods. Read the story and answer questions 17 through 21.

Out of the Woods*

There was a strange silence in the woods. As they walked, Gabriel and Marie could hear birds chirping, pine needles crunching under their feet, the snapping of twigs, even the slight thump of the occasional pine cone landing softly.

They had been hiking as part of a project with their natural sciences class, a group that included thirteen other students and two teachers. As the trail became steeper, the others had started to fall behind. Mr. Davis had kept up with Gabriel and Marie most of the way, but had turned around to make sure the others were on the right track. Oblivious to the group, Gabriel and Marie had climbed and climbed as the trail narrowed and twisted and peaked.

"It's the soccer legs," said Gabriel, who was a forward on the varsity team. "I could climb forever."

"You'll be sore tomorrow," said Marie. "I, on the other hand, have the stamina. I'm used to logging miles and miles." Marie ran cross-country.

"Miles of flat land. We'll see who's sore tomorrow."

They thought they had been following a straight course, but when they finally turned back to find the group, they discovered that the trail had actually split.

"Are we lost?" Marie asked.

"How could we be lost? They were all here just a few minutes ago."

The sheer silence, the absence of other human voices, was overwhelming.

"Let's go back that way." Marie pointed at the trail leading in the opposite direction.

The trail led nowhere. Gabriel and Marie soon found themselves at a precipice, looking down into a canyon. Realizing that they were lost, they panicked. Every snap of a twig was a mountain lion stalking them; every twitch of a branch behind them was a bear getting ready to charge. They ran. They ran wildly, blindly into the forest ahead, slipping on pine needles, leaping over fallen branches, and looking— they later agreed, laughing—like complete idiots.

"You should have seen yourself," said Marie. She mimicked a terrified face.

"Me? You're the one who ran into a tree," said Gabriel.

"I tripped!"

"Okay, you just keep saying that." Gabriel looked around. "We can't be too far from everyone."

"Then why can't we hear them?"

They followed the trail back and began to make their way down the mountain. Surely they could find their way to the beginning of the trail. As they hiked down, the landscape looked unfamiliar. "Hey, this doesn't look

right," said Gabriel, stopping. "Look how the trail slopes up again."

"We didn't come this way."

"Let's go back," said Gabriel.

"No, wait. Listen." Both were quiet. They heard a sound, a new sound.

"It's a creek!" The first trail had crossed over a creek!

The sound of water led them to the creek. Following the direction of the running water, they hiked along the creek bed until they reached another trail crossing.

"This is it!"

"I knew we'd find it," said Marie. They jumped the creek and ran down the trail. As the trail widened, they ran even faster, propelled by relief. Nearing the road where the bus was parked, they heard the sounds they had been longing to hear.

"Come on," yelled Gabriel. "Race!"

17. What is the author's purpose in writing this story?

A   to entertain the reader with a lesson about paying attention to the surroundings when hiking

B   to teach the reader a moral about the importance of listening to your leader

C   to present factual information about the best places in nature to hike

D   to give an explanation of what to take when preparing to go for a hike

18. Read this sentence from the selection.

> Every snap of a twig was a mountain lion stalking them; every twitch of a branch behind them was a bear getting ready to charge.

What does the author convey in the above sentence?

A   Although the woods had been strangely silent at first, now they were full of deafening noises.

B   The strange noises Gabriel and Marie heard were being made by different animals.

C   Every strange noise they heard was frightening to Gabriel and Marie.

D   The woods were full of dangerous animals that were stalking Gabriel and Marie.

19. Read this sentence from the selection.

> Nearing the road where the bus was parked, they heard the sounds they had been longing to hear.

In this sentence, the author is referring to the sounds of—

A   the voices of the other hikers.

B   the water in the creek.

C   the pine needles crunching under their feet.

D   the noises of other cars on the road where the bus was parked.

20. How do Marie and Gabriel react when they discover that they are lost?

A   Gabriel is confident but Marie is afraid.

B   Marie is confident but Gabriel is afraid.

C   Marie and Gabriel are both confident.

D   Marie and Gabriel are both afraid.

21. Gabriel and Marie's relationship is best described as _____.

A   competitive

B   supportive

C   indifferent

D   unconcerned

The following article provides information about a potentially fatal source of food that koalas were given in zoos. Read the article and answer questions 22 through 26.

Deadly Leaves*

Koalas, native to the Australian wilds, initially proved difficult to keep alive in zoos. Because koalas eat nothing but the leaves of the eucalyptus tree, zoos provided them with an unlimited supply of eucalyptus leaves. One zoo even planted eucalyptus trees in a special grove to ensure that the koalas had a continual supply of fresh leaves. However, koalas kept in captivity always died within a year of their arrival at the zoo.

Eventually it was discovered that eucalyptus trees that are less than five years old sometimes generate hydrocyanic acid in their leaves. Taking in small quantities of this acid is fatal to the koala. In their natural habitat, the koalas' senses tell them which eucalyptus trees have dangerous leaves, and they simply move on to other trees until they find leaves that are safe to eat. But in captivity, when their keepers unknowingly were giving them leaves contaminated with acid, the koalas were left with only two options: eat the poisonous leaves or starve. Either option was fatal to the trapped koalas.

Fortunately, today's zoos use special tests to distinguish between poisonous eucalyptus leaves and safe ones, and now koalas are eating well and thriving in zoos.

22. **What does the word *contaminated* mean in the following phrase?**

> But in captivity, when their keepers unknowingly were giving them leaves contaminated with acid, the koalas were left with only two options: eat the poisonous leaves or starve.

A carried with

B polished with

C poisoned with

D grown from

23. **What is the purpose of this article?**

A to inform

B to persuade

C to entertain

D to express opinion

24. **What tone does the author establish in the article?**

A critical

B hopeful

C straightforward

D humorous

25. **What was ironic in this article?**

A Some zoos planted cucalyptus trees for koalas.

B People who were supposed to take care of koalas were accidentally poisoning them.

C Koalas only eat eucalyptus leaves.

D Now koalas are doing much better in zoos.

26. **The _____ tone of this article makes it easy to believe.**

A energetic

B unrealistic

C serious

D persuasive

The following document is from a training manual for new employees at a restaurant. Read the document and answer questions 27 through 31.

Staff Responsibilities*

Greeter

Your job as restaurant greeter requires that you greet every guest graciously and promptly. Upon greeting our early Sunset diners*, be sure to provide them with the regular dinner menu as well as the special Sunset menu. In addition, every evening the chef posts daily specials on the chalkboard at the entrance. Be sure to remind the customers of those dishes too, although those are not eligible for the early Sunset dinner price. (Diners who are seated after the early Sunset period should not receive the special Sunset menu.)

You will be working with a team of three additional members: the person who sets the table and provides the water and place settings (in some restaurants referred to as the busboy or busgirl), the waiter/waitress who actually takes each order to the exact specification of each diner, and the cashier who will accept the diners' payments upon their way out the door after dining. Your job is to ensure that the diners feel welcomed, informed, and served pleasantly in every possible way. For example, if their coats are draped across the back of their chairs, creating a potential floor hazard, please suggest that you would be happy to hang them in the closet at the rear of the restaurant.

Our goal is satisfied, happy customers who will return to visit us again and will recommend our establishment to their friends. Each employee plays an important role in ensuring that our goal is met. If you smile, greet diners pleasantly, seat them as soon as possible, and provide them with the full range of dinner options, you should have every reason to believe that you have done your job well.

When customers have been unhappy in the past with the quality of service by the person who filled your position, it was generally because of one of the following reasons:

- Customers were left standing in the foyer as the entry greeter continued a personal phone call, ignoring them.

- Customers were not told of their eligibility or ineligibility for the early Sunset dinner.

- Customers' seating preferences were not honored.

---

* Early Sunset definition: a choice from one of five set-price, three-course meals available to diners seated before 6:00 PM, Monday through Friday. Note: One of those choices is always vegetarian.

27. **What is the purpose of this selection?**

    A to notify customers of Sunset dinner rules

    B to describe the layout of the restaurant and kitchen

    C to explain the duties of the greeter

    D to make new employees aware of meal prices

28. **The document provides the MOST information on—**

    A how to satisfy diners.

    B how to get along with coworkers.

    C the restaurant's special offers.

    D the restaurant's payment policy.

29. **Read this sentence from the selection.**

    > Your job as a restaurant greeter requires that you greet each guest graciously and promptly.

    According to this sentence, what must greeters do?

    A Welcome customers warmly as they arrive.

    B Quickly list the specials for the customers.

    C Ask the customers what they would like to drink.

    D Seat customers as soon as possible.

30. **The document provides the LEAST information on—**

    A Sunset specials.

    B food preparation.

    C greeter responsibilities.

    D customer dissatisfaction.

31. **The purpose of the three bulleted items at the end of the reading is to—**

    A welcome new employees.

    B help new employees avoid common mistakes.

    C inform new employees of their rights.

    D train new employees to put customers' coats away.

The following is a brochure provided for new volunteers at a pet hospital. Read the brochure and answer questions 32 through 36.

Pet Hospital*

Being a volunteer pet-aide in the Community Pet Hospital should be lots of fun! You were selected among many other applicants; so, you should feel proud that we recognize that you have something special to offer—a passion for helping pets in need. We also hope that over your eight-week assignment with us you will develop useful skills that will serve you well when you seek employment in the future. Who knows? Perhaps you will want to become a veterinarian too someday!

The pets who come to Community Pet Hospital are experiencing some level of illness, injury, or behavioral distress. Since we limit our practice to reptiles and birds, we can somewhat predict the activity in our waiting room on a typical day.

Frankly, we have more problems with pet owners than with the pets themselves. You will notice that we have signs prominently hanging around the office asking that owners should not release their pets from their pens or cages while in the office. Yet, nearly everyday some owner will permit his or her pet to crawl or fly about the office anyway. As a volunteer pet-aide, we ask you to discourage owners from this practice. But if and when it happens, we appreciate your assistance in helping to retrieve the escaped pet.

When pets and their owners are being seated, we ask your assistance in separating, when possible, the birds from the reptiles. This can help prevent a noisy, distressing climate in the waiting room. Also, it is our experience that small birds need separation from large birds who tend to be aggressive and dominate the "chatter."

While we only have a few snakes in our practice, their visits can provoke upsetting responses in the waiting room. Both pets and owners seem to respond poorly to the presence of snakes in the waiting room, even if they are caged. So our receptionist tries very hard to arrange snake appointments at the end of the day when most of our other patients have been seen and are gone.

We encourage your interest in every pet that comes through the door! However, there are a few basic rules in engaging with any pet patient that are essential for you to apply at all times:

1. The pet owner should be politely asked first if it is acceptable to interact with his or her pet.

2. Don't assume that a pet wants to interact with anyone except his or her owner. You may like the pet but it may not like you (or anyone else).

3. Refrain from physically handling any pet except as absolutely necessary. Pets who come to us are in distress, so additional handling by strangers may exacerbate their fragile condition.

4. Pets in distress may lash out in self-defense and could injure you with a bite or a painful scratch.

5. Excessive attention paid to one pet may make an owner of another pet somewhat jealous on the other side of the room.

6. Sometimes it seems that paying attention to a pet causes an owner to feel it is all right to open the pen or cage in order to demonstrate pet tricks. We don't want that!

7. In the event you do handle any pet in any way, immediately wash your hands well with disinfectant soap in the washroom. *Absolutely never* touch one pet immediately after handling another unless your hands are thoroughly cleaned between interactions.

Helping a pet in distress and its owner is a very rewarding experience. We're sure you will come to feel the satisfaction of your contributions to the harmony of our waiting room here at the Community Pet Hospital.

32. What does *retrieve* mean as used in the following sentence?

> But if and when it happens, we appreciate your assistance in helping to retrieve the escaped pet.

A help take care of the pet

B help the owners take care of the pet

C help the pet escape and leave the office

D help catch the pet and put it back into its cage

33. Which of the following is NOT a correct rewording of the following sentence?

> Additional handling by strangers may exacerbate its fragile condition.

A A stranger handling a pet may worsen its condition.

B A stranger handling a pet may improve its condition.

C A stranger handling a pet may intensify its condition.

D A stranger handling a pet may aggravate its condition.

34. The main purpose of this brochure is—

A to explain to veterinarians how to care for hurt animals.

B to explain to pet owners how to care for reptiles and birds.

C to explain why pet owners should use the Community Pet Hospital.

D to explain how volunteers should interact with pet patients and their owners.

35. Which of the following is NOT discussed in this brochure?

A how snake appointments are made by the receptionist

B how to release pets from their pens or cages while in the office

C why small birds need separating from large birds

D why the hospital can predict the activity in the waiting room on a typical day

36. Which of these sentences from the reading best describes the main idea (thesis)?

A Being a volunteer pet aide in the Community Pet Hospital should be lots of fun!

B The pets who come to Community Pet Hospital are experiencing some level of illness, injury, or behavioral distress.

C Frankly, we have more problems with pet owners than with the pets themselves.

D We're sure you will come to feel the satisfaction of your contributions to the harmony of our waiting room here at the Community Pet Hospital.

The following essay discusses the early years of the film industry. Read the essay and answer questions 37 through 41.

On Screen*

The lights go down and flickering images appear on the big screen. Suddenly, the engaging grins of two small boys emerge in black and white. The tow-headed boys are dressed in coveralls and are sitting on a porch with their dusty bare feet propped on a wooden step below them. A long-eared hound lies listlessly at their feet. Catcalls and giggles fill the theater. "Hey, look. It's George and Roy. And there's old Tige snoozin' away at their feet." Applause and more giggles break out in the small movie house in eastern Tennessee.

It is early in the twentieth century, and movie houses are springing up all over the country. During this time, nickelodeons were being replaced by a new industry. The emerging movie houses were given regal names such as the "Majestic," the "Imperial," and the "Plaza." Patrons were happy to pay the price of a movie ticket, usually 10 cents, to see the latest moving picture show. At first, single reels of film were projected onto the big screen. By 1907, multiple reels of film were spliced together and presented as feature films. Early audiences were lured into the movie houses not only by the western feature shown every Saturday but also by the promise of seeing still shots of themselves up on the big screen.

Traveling photographers earned a living, moving from town to town, taking photos of local people— especially children—and nearby scenes of interest to show on the screen of the local movie house. The photographers were paid not only by the movie house owner who knew that local shots would be popular attractions, but they were also paid by the parents for the children's photographs. Eventually, these still shots of local people and places were replaced by newsreels of current news events, such as the world wars in Europe. These newsreels, precursors of the evening news now watched nightly, showed flickering images of real men going off to battle. The reels played before the main feature and were eagerly awaited reports of current events in the world.

The early features shown every Saturday and occasionally during the week were silent films. A local, talented pianist usually sat in the front of the theater supplying a musical backdrop for the action. Chords were pounded out as the western film star Tom Mix rode his horse up to the latest, staged train robbery or as the Keystone Cops investigated another caper.

Soon, the feature films were no longer silent; recorded sound was now possible, and the feature films were now referred to as "talkies" and became even more popular. The films were all in black and white, with color films not appearing until the late 1930s.

With the invention of air conditioning, movie theaters became cool retreats in the midst of summer's sultriest weather. The Rivoli Theater in New York heavily advertised the cool comfort of the interior, and summer ticket sales soared. Eager patrons slipped in out of the heat and humidity and enjoyed the cooled air and watched the latest feature film.

Today, movie theaters remain cool havens of sight and sound entertainment. Popcorn and sodas are served in every theater—multiplexes showing several different features at once. Missing are the still photographs of local children or scenes. The only remaining clues as to their part in the development of the industry are faded copies of the original photographs now tucked away in dusty family albums.

37. **The main idea of this essay is that movies—**

    A   are popular because theaters are air conditioned.

    B   provide audiences with world news.

    C   give parents an opportunity to entertain children.

    D   have been entertaining audiences for many years.

38. **Which of the following sentences from the essay helps describe the setting of the opening paragraph?**

    A   "Nickelodeons were being replaced by a new industry."

    B   "The films were all in black and white, with color films not appearing until the late 1930s."

    C   "Patrons were happy to pay the price of a movie ticket, usually ten cents, to see the latest moving picture show."

    D   "The lights go down and flickering images appear on the big screen."

39. **Why did the movie theaters show still pictures of local people?**

    A   because they also showed silent films

    B   because the films were in black and white

    C   to attract audiences

    D   to sell more popcorn and sodas

40. **Which phrase from the reading refers back to early 20th century movies?**

    A   "faded copies of the original photographs"

    B   "theaters became cool retreats"

    C   "recorded sound was now possible"

    D   "flickering images of real men going off to battle"

41. **What is the tone of this informative article?**

    A   sympathetic

    B   sarcastic

    C   objective

    D   critical

The following article tells of children seining for minnows while also offering some general information on the fish. Read the article and answer questions 42 through 45.

Seining for Minnows*

There was a time when hot summer days brought children outdoors to local creeks and streambeds to seine for minnows. Catching the small, silver fish was a fun, refreshing opportunity to wade in cool, rushing water on a sultry summer's day. Before setting out for the creek in their neighborhood, however, children first had to locate a burlap bag to use for a seine. Girls as well as boys loved this outdoor activity.

Upon reaching the creek bank, the children pulled off their socks and shoes and plunged feet first into the cold, sparkling water. Wading carefully over the pebbly bottom, they looked for the right spot where the minnows flashed. Seining for minnows was easiest if two children worked together. Grasping two corners of the bag, each child would stand in shallow water and slowly lower the bag until it was flat on the bottom of the streambed. Then, standing very still, the children would wait for the dirt and silt to settle and for the fish life in the stream to resume normal activity. The children would bend over and again grasp a corner of the bag in each hand and quickly and smoothly raise the bag straight up, keeping it as level as possible. A flutter and flicker of silver shades would glimmer all over the soaked burlap bag. Dozens of tiny silver fish almost too small to have been seen in the stream would now cover the rough bag. Tiny little fish bodies, startled by being thrust into the open air, would wiggle and turn, seeking an outlet back into the cold, clear water of their creek.

The joy of seining for minnows is that, once caught, the fish are thrown back into the water to continue their natural lives, perhaps to be scooped up by other children and then returned again to their watery home. So the net is swiftly lowered back into the stream, and the small fish swim off. Then the whole process is repeated once more as more minnows are scooped up and then released.

The small silver fish that children call minnows are really any small fish, regardless of species. Fish called *minnows* actually belong to the *cyprindae* family of fish. Members of the *cyprindae* family, including carp and goldfish among several dozen species, can be found in lakes and streams throughout the United States and much of the world.

Minnows often serve as primary consumers in a streambed, sometimes as bottom feeders to suck up ooze or eat algae. Others, as secondary consumers, ingest zooplankton, crustaceans, insects, worms, and other minnows. Some become food for tertiary consumers, being the prey of birds, mammals, and other fish. Those of a larger size are used as bait for sport fishing. Still others are used as food additives in livestock feeds.

Their role as prey and their use as bait and food additives are not the only dangers that minnows face in the world today. The child with a burlap sack who goes out to seine for minnows on a summer's day now will find fewer glittering fish on the bag when it is lifted out of the stream. The destruction and alteration of the minnows' habitat due to land treatment and watercourse alteration threaten the future of this beautiful, hardy family of fish. If the children of tomorrow are to have the joy of seining for minnows on a hot summer's day, the natural habitats of our lakes and streams must be preserved.

42. What does the word *consumers* mean in the following sentence?

> Minnows often serve as primary consumers in a streambed, sometimes as bottom feeders to suck up ooze or eat algae.

A those who shop

B those who eat

C those who occupy

D those who serve

43. This article suggests that minnows face which of the following dangers?

A being used as prey or bait

B eating poisonous food

C lack of food

D children playing in the water

44. What information supports the idea that minnows play an important role in the food chain?

A Minnows do not eat algae.

B Minnows only eat worms and insects.

C Birds avoid eating minnows.

D Birds and other minnows eat minnows.

45. Which of the following items is closest in meaning to the word "seine" as used in this story?

> …however, the children first had to locate a burlap bag to use as a seine.

A backpack

B paper bag

C bucket

D net

The following article discusses the inspiring efforts of Esther Morris in her crusade for women's suffrage. Read the article and answer questions 46 through 48.

A One-Woman Campaign*

In the territory of Wyoming on September 6, 1870, for the first time anywhere in the United States, women went to the polls to cast their ballots. By 1870, the women's suffrage movement had battled unsuccessfully for 30 years on the East Coast. The big surprise to everyone was that the first victory for women's right to vote occurred in Wyoming, where there had been no public speeches, rallies, or conventions for the women's suffrage movement. Instead, there had been just one remarkable woman: Esther Morris. Her one-woman campaign is a classic example of effective politics. She managed to persuade both rival candidates in a territorial election to promise that, if elected, they would introduce a bill for women's suffrage. She knew that, as long as the winner kept his word, women's suffrage would score a victory in Wyoming. The winning candidate kept his promise to Esther Morris, which led to this historic Wyoming voting event in 1870.

46. According to the article, why is it surprising that Wyoming was the first state to allow women to vote?

    A Few people knew about formal elections.

    B There was a small population of women in the state.

    C The community showed no obvious interest in the issue.

    D The efforts on the East Coast were moving ahead quickly.

47. Which statement below BEST illustrates the time sequence of the events in the article?

    A It begins in the present and then goes back in time to explain the preceding events.

    B It begins on September 6, 1870 and then goes back in time to explain the preceding events.

    C It begins in 1865 and moves to September 6, 1870 and then goes back to 1865.

    D It all takes place on the same day—September 6, 1870.

48. Which sentence from the article explains specifically how Esther Morris succeeded in providing the women of Wyoming with the right to vote?

    A "The big surprise to everyone was that the first victory for women's right to vote occurred in Wyoming, where there were no public speeches, rallies, or conventions for the women's suffrage movement."

    B "In the territory of Wyoming on September 6, 1870, for the first time anywhere in the United States, women went to the polls to cast their ballots."

    C "She managed to persuade both rival candidates in a territorial election to promise that, if elected, they would introduce a bill for women's suffrage."

    D "She knew that, as long as the winner kept his word, women's suffrage would score a victory in Wyoming."

The following is a rough draft of an essay discussing how opposite sides of the writer's brain might influence her personality and behavior. It may contain errors in grammar, punctuation, sentence structure, and organization. Some of the questions may refer to underlined or numbered sentences or phrases within the text. Read the essay and answer questions 49 through 51.

My Brain*

Sometimes I think I am probably more right-brained, but other times I feel more left-brained. I love to play music and I especially like to make it up as I go along. For anybody else to hear my music, they might think it sounds like noise. (1) My brother, for one, always complains about it.

I also like to write poetry. It is a way for me to put down on paper how I am really feeling. I write things in my poetry I would probably never tell anyone else. I am also pretty good at giving prepared speeches in my English class. Because I really like to do these kinds of things, I feel that I must be right-brained.

But there are other times I am not so sure about it. For example, I am really pretty good at math and other things that require me to be logical. I also think I am pretty good at writing essays about technical things, like explaining how things work. And I'm good at remembering things too. (2)

Though I guess I prefer right-brained activities and can do them more easily, I can do left-brained things pretty well if I have to. I like doing math problems. So I am not sure what that makes me!

49. **Which of the following sentences does NOT fit well in the paragraph in which it is found?**

   A "I love to play music and I especially like to make it up as I go along." (first paragraph)

   B "I also like to write poetry." (second paragraph)

   C "I like doing math problems." (fourth paragraph)

   D "For example, I am really pretty good at math and other things that require me to be logical." (third paragraph)

50. **What is the BEST way to rewrite the underlined sentence marked (1)?**

   A For anybody else to hear my music, he might think it sounds like noise.

   B For anybody else to hear my music, she might think it sounds like noise.

   C For other people to hear my music, they might think it sounds like noise.

   D Leave as is

51. **What is the BEST way to combine the underlined sentences labeled (2)?**

   A I am good at writing technical essays explaining how things work, and I also have a good memory.

   B Writing technical essays, I am good at explaining how things work and have a good memory.

   C I am good at explaining how things work by writing technical essays and remembering things too.

   D Explaining how things work and technical things are things I am good at writing essays about, and I have a good memory.

The following is a rough draft of an article suggesting that water may have flowed (or does flow) on the planet Mars. It may contain errors in grammar, punctuation, sentence structure, and organization. The question may refer to numbered sentences or phrases within the text. Read the article and answer question 52.

Water on Mars*

(1) For a long time, people have considered the possibility that life may have once existed (or may still exist) on the planet Mars. (2) In 1910, Percival Lowell wrote a book suggesting that a large system of "canals" was built on Mars by a civilization that has since disappeared. (3) The "canals" were grooves on the planet's surface which Lowell saw through a telescope he believed had been built by Martians. (4) We now know that Lowell was wrong—there is no evidence of construction on Mars. (5) However, recent photos from the Mars Orbiter Camera suggest that, until very recently, liquid water flowed on the surface of the planet. (6) And some scientists believe that liquid water might still be found beneath the planet's surface. (7) Why is this important? (8) Well, scientists think that water is necessary for life to develop. (9) If there was (or is) water on Mars, it's quite possible that the planet may have supported life at some point during its history. (10) And if there was once life on Mars, the odds that there is life elsewhere in the Universe become much greater. (11) Scientists warn that it's too early to tell for sure, but maybe we Earthlings are not alone after all.

52. **What is the correct way to express the ideas in the sentence labeled (3)?**

   A When the "canals" were observed by Lowell, he believed that they had been built by Martians through his telescope.

   B The "canals" were grooves on the planet's surface that, when observed by Lowell, appeared to have been built by Martians.

   C Through a telescope, Martians were those who Lowell believed had built the "canals."

   D Leave as is.

The following is a rough draft of an essay that discusses the future of the human race in light of the Earth's history. It may contain errors in grammar, punctuation, sentence structure, and organization. Some of the questions may refer to underlined or numbered sentences or phrases within the text. Read the essay and answer questions 53 through 56.

Killer Asteroids*

People tend to think that the human race will be around forever. After all, we have been here for thousands of years and, many would argue, we dominate our planet in a way that no other species ever has. However, before we get too cocky, it would be wise to review the history of the Earth. Many species before us have enjoyed great success only to fall victim to changes in climate, <u>competing of</u> (1) other species, or other factors beyond their control. Could the same thing happen to human beings?

Just as humans do today, dinosaurs once walked the Earth in great numbers. Then, about 65 million years ago, an asteroid about 5 to 10 miles across hit the Earth and everything changed. The asteroid produced a deadly fireball, threw huge amounts of dust into the atmosphere, and caused tidal waves, fires, and terrible storms. With their world so <u>interestingly</u> (2) changed, the dinosaurs were helpless. And most scientists agree that it is only a matter of time before another asteroid hits the Earth, causing similar <u>trouble</u>. (3)

Of course, humans might have a better chance of survival than the dinosaurs did. We can adapt to a wide range of climates, and <u>even underground living is something</u> <u>we can do if</u> <u>we have to</u>. (4) We might even be able to use our technology to locate the asteroid and destroy it before it strikes the Earth. However, there is one thing about which everyone can agree. If human beings ever have to face a killer asteroid from space, it is our brains rather than our brawn that will give us a fighting chance.

53. **Which phrase would BEST replace the underlined phrase labeled (1)?**

    A competed by

    B competition from

    C compete by

    D Leave as is.

54. **To more accurately describe how the impact of the asteroid changed the dinosaurs' world, the underlined word labeled (2) should be changed to—**

    A dramatically.

    B strangely.

    C mysteriously.

    D thrillingly.

55. **In order to achieve more precise meaning, the underlined word labeled (3) should be changed to—**

    A danger.

    B worry.

    C destruction.

    D hassle.

56. **Which change to the underlined clause labeled (4) would make it more consistent with the first part of the sentence?**

    A even underground living can be done by us if we have to.

    B even we can live underground if we have to.

    C we can even live underground if we have to.

    D Leave as is.

The following is part of a rough draft of a paragraph about visiting another country, specifically China. It may contain mistakes in grammar, punctuation, sentence structure, or organization. Read the article and answer the questions 57 through 59.

International Travel 101

The often-overlooked differences, such as dining etiquette, names and titles, and attitude towards foreigners can be (1) <u>very</u> important (2) <u>to knowing</u> on a visit to China. Little things like understanding dining protocol can turn an otherwise confusing situation into an enjoyable learning experience. Knowing the correct way to address a new acquaintance can make an awkward situation flow smoothly. Likewise, coming prepared with the knowledge of the citizens' general reaction to foreigners will help dispel any unnecessary fears or embarrassment. A country, much like a puzzle, is a complete idea made up of many different bits and pieces. Knowing how the pieces fit together is essential to (3) <u>understanding and appreciating</u> the beauty of the whole.

57. **What is the best way to express the idea of the underlined word labeled (1)?**

   A   so

   B   that

   C   excessively

   D   lcavc as is

58. **What is the correct way to write the underlined phrase labeled (2)?**

   A   to know

   B   to be known

   C   to have known

   D   leave as is

59. **What is the best way to write the underlined phrase labeled (3)?**

   A   understanding and appreciate

   B   understand and appreciating

   C   understanding and to appreciate

   D   leave as is

Read this piece of dramatic literature and answer questions 60 through 62.

Sea Symphony

She sits there on the waterfront

smiling at the sky

the tide comes up to kiss her hem

the clouds just float on by

5   A basket of the finest shells

is resting near her hip

a perfect spiral held aloft

an ocean cave within

You wonder what she's looking at

10   to make her shine so bright

you've watched her for awhile now

her laughter your delight

So ask her what she's feeling

and hold her hand quite tight

15   then you shall know the symphony

of wind of waves and light.

60. **What does "a perfect spiral" refer to?**

   A a picture

   B a cloud

   C an orchestra

   D a seashell

61. **The phrase "shine so bright" gives a feeling of _____.**

   A happiness

   B intelligence

   C popularity

   D youthfulness

62. **This style of writing is an example of what kind of dramatic literature?**

   A a poem

   B an essay

   C a short story

   D a play

For questions 63 through 68, choose the answer that is the most effective substitute for each underlined part of the sentence. If no substitution is necessary, choose "Leave as is."

63. When Tom <u>arrived at school he</u> was carrying all his books with him.

    A arrived at school, he

    B arrived, at school he

    C arrived at school he,

    D Leave as is.

64. <u>After, the volcano erupted, the</u> tiny tropical island was quiet and devastated.

    A After the volcano erupted, the

    B After the volcano erupted the

    C After the volcano erupts, the

    D Leave as is.

65. Responsibilities of the job include <u>greeting customers, escorting them to a table, and offering beverages.</u>

    A greeting customers, escort them to a table and offer a beverage.

    B to greet customers, escorting them to tables and offering a beverage.

    C to greet customers, escorting them to a table, and to offer a beverage.

    D Leave as is.

66. <u>A dog bit Tom's ankle while riding a bicycle.</u>

    A Riding a bicycle, a dog bit Tom's ankle.

    B While riding a bicycle, a dog bit Tom's ankle.

    C While Tom was riding a bicycle, a dog bit his ankle.

    D Leave as is.

67. <u>When the money was stolen by the bandits, the owner</u> of the store felt betrayed.

    A When the bandits stole the money, the owner

    B The money was stolen by the bandits. The owner

    C By the bandits the money was stolen. The owner

    D Leave as is.

68. <u>The poetry of Langston Hughes combining</u> the idioms of African-American speech and the rhythms of the blues.

    A The poetry of Langston Hughes will combine

    B The poetry of Langston Hughes combines

    C Langston Hughes' poetry combining

    D Leave as is.

For questions 69 through 72, choose the word or phrase that best completes the sentence.

69. "We should _____ without the captain," the coach said impatiently.

    A proceeds

    B precede

    C precedent

    D proceed

70. The legendary goddess was the _____ of all the Greek deities.

    A beautifulest

    B more beautiful

    C most beautiful

    D most beautifying

71. The frightened pilot's face was ashen as he gingerly lowered the plane onto the Smiths' private _____ that time was running out for his ailing friend.

    A runway: he knew

    B runway, he knew

    C runway. He knew

    D runway but he knew

72. "Which of the three Olympic runners is the _____?" the spectator asked the judge.

    A more fast

    B fastest

    C most fastest

    D most faster

Writing Task:*

By the time students enter high school, they have learned about many moments in history that have influenced our world today. Think about a moment in history you studied and consider its importance.

Write a composition in which you discuss a moment in history. Share its importance in today's world. Be sure to support the moment with details and examples.

Checklist for Your Writing

The following checklist will help you do your best work. Make sure you:

❑ Read the description of the task carefully.

❑ Use specific details and examples to fully support your ideas.

❑ Organize your writing with a strong introduction, body, and conclusion.

❑ Choose specific words that are appropriate for your audience and purpose.

❑ Vary your sentences to make your writing interesting to read.

❑ Check for mistakes in grammar, spelling, punctuation, and sentence formation.

STOP

Note: The following questions for Practice Test 1 are reprinted, by permission, from California High School Exit Exam (CAHSEE), California Department of Education, P.O. Box 271, Sacramento, CA 95812-0271: 1, 2, 3, 6, 7, 8, 12, 13, 14, 17, 18, 19, 22, 23, 24, 27, 28, 29, 30, 32, 33, 34, 35, 37, 38, 42, 43, 44, 46, 47, 48, 49, 51, 52, 53, 54, 55, 56, 63, 64, 65, 66, 67, 68, 69, 70, 71, 72.

Answer Key

1.	B	25.	B	49.	C
2.	A	26.	C	50.	C
3.	D	27.	C	51.	A
4.	D	28.	A	52.	B
5.	A	29.	A	53.	B
6.	A	30.	B	54.	A
7.	B	31.	B	55.	C
8.	C	32.	D	56.	C
9.	D	33.	B	57.	D
10.	B	34.	D	58.	A
11.	C	35.	B	59.	D
12.	A	36.	D	60.	D
13.	C	37.	D	61.	A
14.	A	38.	D	62.	A
15.	D	39.	C	63.	A
16.	B	40.	A	64.	A
17.	A	41.	A	65.	D
18.	C	42.	B	66.	C
19.	A	43.	A	67.	A
20.	D	44.	D	68.	B
21.	A	45.	D	69.	D
22.	C	46.	C	70.	C
23.	A	47.	B	71.	C
24.	C	48.	C	72.	B

Detailed Explanations of Answers

PRACTICE TEST 1

1. **B**

"Over the horizon" is an example of figurative language that implies great distance. The expression "disappear... forever" implies abandonment. (A), (C), and (D) are incorrect; they are all temporary conditions.

2. **A**

In this article, (B) and (C) are in the story but not mentioned as a reason why falconers enjoy the sport, and (D) is not mentioned in the article. Choice (A) is the best summary.

3. **D**

The whole third paragraph focuses on the rewards of falconry, so the author obviously thinks it is a rewarding sport. (A) and (B) are not stated or implied in the reading, and (C) is an incorrect reading of the text. Peregrine falcons are mentioned as an example but not singled out as the *best*.

4. **D**

Seeing a falcon disappear forever would be a sad experience. (A) is the opposite meaning, (B) implies no emotion at all, and (C) *sarcastic* is incorrect because the tone of the article is upbeat and positive.

5. **A**

This story shows a *contradiction* between being a wild animal and becoming tame enough to *trust* people. (B) means *unclear*, (C) means *mildly*, (D) means an old way of doing things, and none of these answers is appropriate to the meaning of the sentence.

6. **A**

This is a tricky question. (A) is correct because the return of a portion of the purchase price is a *rebate*. (B), tax credits, may in fact be the method the government uses to provide these rebates, but it is not mentioned in the article. (C) and (D) do not make sense in this context, because this part of the article is about "financial and time-saving benefits for the drivers."

7. **B**

The word "populated" in the article implies that with more people, we use more resources. (A) and (C) are clearly incorrect from the context. (D) is closer to the truth, but not as clear and specific as (B).

8. **C**

Choice (A) is one of the ideas in the article, but not the main one because not much space is devoted to it. Choice (B) contains an idea that is not included in the reading at all. Choice (D) is a general topic that this article falls under, but is not specific enough to be the main idea. All of the article works together to support the idea listed in (C).

9. **D**

The first paragraph provides some alarming information designed to get the attention of the reader. Choices (A) and (C) are incorrect because this paragraph does not even mention electric cars, the main idea of the article, and it only includes general statements, so (B) is also not a good answer.

10. **B**

Conversely indicates *contrast* or *opposition.* "Furthermore" (A) shows *addition,* "for example" (C) indicates that an *example* will follow, and "consequently" (D) means that a *result* will follow. Only (B), "on the other hand," shows *contrast,* so it is the best answer.

11. **C**

"To give out" has the meaning of "to stop working after being used for a long time" and applies to the "body of an electric car." "Goes out" (A) has a similar meaning but applies only to items with working parts such as an automobile engine, or even some part of the human body: "His back went out." (B) means to *omit,* and (D) means to *try to obtain a position,* especially on a sports team. "Wears out" (C) has a similar meaning to "gives out," so it is the best answer.

12. **A**

Eccentric means *unusual.* Choice (B), large population, is not included in the reading. According to the article, Choices (C) and (D) are also characteristics of California, but neither of them has the same meaning as *eccentricities.* Vocabulary flash cards are a good idea for words like this one.

13. **C**

The key points in this article are the geography, the population, and the unusual features of the state. (A) is a descriptive detail that supports the point about California's geography, (B) introduces the point about the unusual features of the state, and (D) introduces the point about California's population. Only (C) *directly* supports the theme, or main idea, of the article.

14. Ⓐ

"Imagery" means painting a mental picture, and the author does this throughout the article, from "snow-capped mountains" to "black and yellow Monarch butterflies." Choices (B) and (C) are incorrect because there are no statistics (numbers) and no quoting of experts in the article. (D) is incorrect because there are no historical facts in the article—all of the description is of the present time.

15. Ⓓ

Words like *majestically*, *golden*, *fragrant*, *beauty*, *richness*, and *magic* show very clearly the enthusiasm that the author wishes to communicate. Choice (A) is not strong enough, and Choices (B) and (C) are not correct because there is no doubtful, questioning, or negative feeling in the article.

16. Ⓑ

As in Question 15, the glowing descriptive vocabulary in the article shows the author's positive feelings about California, and so does the final sentence. There is nothing in the article to support Choices (A), (C), or (D) (which means *sad*).

17. Ⓐ

The fact that the two hikers were not sure if they had come the way they were returning shows that they should have paid attention to the trail on the way up, and a scary moment that turned out to be funny is entertaining. Choice (B) is incorrect because nowhere in the story does it mention what the leader said. Choices (C) and (D) are not correct because the story does not even mention the best places to hike or what to take on a hiking trip.

18. **C**

This is an example of figurative language, telling us how the noises seemed to Gabriel and Marie rather than how they really were. Choice (A) is incorrect because the noises listed were not loud. Choice (B) is the literal interpretation of this sentence, and Choice (D) is what they believed at the moment, but the context (the words before and after) shows that neither of these was literally true.

19. **A**

Longing means *wanting very much*. Because they had become frightened when they were separated from their group, we can infer that they wanted to hear the sounds of the other members of their group. Choices (B) and (C) have no evidence to support them. Choice (D) is a possibility, but it is not logical to think that they were longing to hear the traffic noise more than the voices of the other hikers, so it is not the best answer.

20. **D**

Clues include words like *overwhelming* and the fact that they both ran from ordinary sounds. If only one of them had run, Choice (A) or (B) might have been correct, and if neither of them had run, then Choice (C) might have been correct.

21. **A**

This answer requires reading between the lines and analyzing the things the hikers said to each other: Both hikers bragged about their physical ability, both hikers made fun of each other, and Gabriel challenged Marie to race. Choice (B) has some truth to it because they both cooperated to get back, but only a few lines in the story mention this, and it is not emphasized. Choices (C) and (D) are not correct because both hikers interacted intensely throughout the story.

22. **C**

This answer makes the most sense. With vocabulary questions like this one, the best strategy is often to try to substitute each of the possible answers. By doing this, we can eliminate Choices (A) and (B) because they do not make sense. Choice (D) is not correct because it is not logical—nobody would use poison to grow leaves with.

23. **A**

This article is full of facts, so it is informative. Choices (B) and (C) are not correct because the article does not ask the reader to do or believe anything, and the topic is certainly not a fun one. Choice (D) is not correct because the information in the story is presented as facts rather than opinions.

24. **C**

The *tone* of the article is the feeling the author communicates. *Straightforward* means *direct* or *to the point*, which is supported by the many facts in the story. Choice (A) is not correct because the author does not criticize the zoos, Choice (B) is not correct because the author does not express hope that the future will be better, and Choice (D) is not correct because there is nothing funny about what happened.

25. **B**

Ironic means that something is the opposite of what is expected. The irony is that the keepers wanted to protect the koalas, but the opposite happened. Choices (A) and (C) are simple facts, and Choice (D) is true but not at all *ironic*.

26. **C**

Both the material in the article and the way it is presented are serious. The article does not come across with a lot of energy, so (A) is not the best answer. The article is realistic because it includes both the good and the bad parts of what happened, so Choice (B) is not correct. Choice (D) is not correct because the story does not try to persuade the reader of anything.

27. **C**

The first clue is the title. The other clue about the purpose of the article is that everything in the article is explaining how to be a good greeter at the restaurant. The article is directed to restaurant employees and not the customers (A). The layout of the kitchen and restaurant is not included (B), and meal prices are not listed (D).

28. **A**

The entire reading is about how to greet customers and make them feel welcome and happy (satisfied). Choices (B) and (D) are not included in the reading. Choice (C) is included, but it is only a small part of the reading, so it is not the best answer.

29. **A**

The correct answer is a paraphrase of the sentence in the box. *Greet* means *welcome*, *graciously* means *warmly*, and *promptly* means *as soon as they arrive*. The specials (B), drinks (C), and seating of customers (D) are not included in this sentence from the reading. Be careful to read the directions carefully ("According to this sentence....") and answer this type of question based on the sentence in the box rather than on the whole reading.

30. **B**

Again, read the question carefully, and notice that it asks for the LEAST information. Skimming the article is a good way to answer this question. Sunset specials are discussed (A), greeter responsibilities are featured all through the reading (C), and how to prevent customer dissatisfaction is also emphasized (D). The only answer not included in the reading is (B).

31. **B**

The paragraph above the bulleted items at the end of the reading tells us that the bulleted items are the reasons that customers were unhappy in the past, so we can infer that their purpose is to help employees provide a happy experience for their guests. It would be illogical to think that they are listed to welcome new employees (A), inform them of their rights (C), or train them to put coats away (D).

32. **D**

This is a vocabulary question. If you don't already know the meaning of *retrieve*, you can try two different strategies. First, the root word *re-* means back, or again, so you can guess that the meaning might be to put the pet *back* in its cage. Second, the word *escaped* in the context implies that the pet should be caught. Answers (A), (B), and (C) are not logical in this situation.

33. **B**

Again, read the question carefully and notice that it asks for the <u>incorrect</u> rewording. The word *exacerbate* means to *make worse or more severe*. Words with similar meanings are *worsen* (A), *intensify* (C), and *aggravate* (D). The best answer is *improve* because it is the only one of the choices with a completely different meaning.

34. **D**

The brochure begins by identifying the audience: "volunteer pet-aide in the Community Pet Hospital...." It is not directed to veterinarians (A) or pet owners (B) and (C). Also, the content of the reading is full of advice for volunteers and how they should relate to the pets and owners.

35. **B**

A good strategy for this type of question is to skim the reading for terms like *snake appointments* (A), *cages* (B), *small birds* and *large birds* (C), and *typical day* (D). When you find one of these terms, read the surrounding information. In this case, you will discover that (A), (C), and (D) are all included in the reading—only (B) is not.

36. **D**

A good strategy here would be to check the beginning and end of the reading first, which narrows our choices to (A) and (D). Most of the brochure is about the contributions the volunteers make and how rewarding that can be. The whole brochure is <u>not</u> about having "lots of fun" (A). Choice (B) is a key point, and (C) is a detail, but neither of them are the main idea of the brochure.

37. **D**

This article talks about movie theaters and audiences in the early part of the 20th Century, and in the 1930s, and more recently (with the invention of air conditioning), and today. Choice (A) is still true today but it is only a detail, Choice (B) is a detail that is no longer true, and Choice (C) is true but is not mentioned in the reading.

38. **D**

The setting of the opening paragraph is a "small movie house in eastern Tennessee," early in the 20th Century, as a picture of two boys and a dog are projected on the screen. Only Choice (D) relates directly to the setting of this first paragraph, although Choices (A), (B), and (C) do provide background information about the setting of the whole first part of the article.

39.

Attract means the same thing as *lure*, which is the reason given in Paragraph 2. Choices (A), (B), and (D) all contain true statements, but none of them tells the <u>reason</u> the theaters showed still pictures.

40.

Find this answer by considering the words "original" and "faded copies," which imply the passing of time. These photographs are now all that is left of an early 20th century practice: showing pictures of local people. Choices (B), (C), and (D) refer to the topic at hand rather than an earlier one in the reading.

41.

The feeling portrayed by the piece is a sympathetic one, with references to fond times spent in movie theaters in the past and today. Nothing in the article supports (B) or (D). Many objective facts (C) are included in the reading, but there are no pros and cons given—just the good points of attending movie theaters.

42.

To *consume* means to *use* or *use up*. In some contexts it could mean shoppers (A) who are out to buy products that they will consume. However, in this context it refers to *feeders*, which means "those who eat." The article points out that minnows do sometimes occupy (C) the bottom of the riverbed, but that is not the meaning of *consumers*. Choice (D) repeats one of the words in the sentence, *serve*, but again does not reflect the meaning of the word *consumers* as used in this sentence.

43. **A**

The dangers mentioned in the article include "their role as prey and their use as bait." The only other danger listed is the destruction of their environment (*habitat*). Choices (B) and (C) are not mentioned in the article. Choice (D) is not really a danger because "once caught, the fish are thrown back into the water to continue their natural lives...."

44. **D**

Choices (A), (B), and (C) are false, according to the reading. Choice (B) includes the word *only*, or it would be true. Only Choice (D) is a true statement, and can be chosen by eliminating the other three answers.

45. **D**

Burlap is a type of loosely woven cloth. Answers (A), (B), and (C) are unsuitable for catching fish in the manner indicated in the story, for the following reasons. A "backpack" (A) would be hard to clean and dry, and probably would not strain the water well. A "paper bag" would become soaked and disintegrate. Answer (C), a "bucket," could be used to catch fish but not to strain them out of the water. "Net" (D) is the best answer because it has the same meaning as *seine*.

46. **C**

Choices (A) and (B) are not mentioned in the article. Choice (D) is not true—the East Coast efforts were "unsuccessful." Choice (C) is a paraphrase of the reasons given in the text, specifically in the sentence that mentions the word *surprise*, so it is the best answer.

47. **B**

The first sentence of this article refers first to events in 1870 and then to the previous 30 years. The article does not mention the present time (A), does not begin in 1865 (C), and even though it begins and ends on September 6, it also refers back to previous events (D).

48.

It is important to read the question carefully. Choice (A) tells how people felt, (B) tells what happened, (D) tells us what Esther Morris knew, but only (C) answers the question by telling specifically *how* she succeeded.

49.

For this question, try to determine the main idea of each paragraph. The first paragraph is about being right-brained and about playing music, so (A) fits. The second paragraph is all about poetry, so (B) fits. The third paragraph is about being good at math and technical things, so (D) fits. The fourth paragraph is the conclusion, and the sentence in Choice (C) should be in paragraph (D) instead of where it is.

50.

Answer (A) is grammatically correct, but the use of the male pronoun "he" seems to imply that "anybody else" refers only to a male. Answer (B) could only be correct when "anybody else" refers to a female. Answer (D) is incorrect because it creates a problem in agreement between "anybody" (singular) and "they" (plural). (Because "anybody else" is an indefinite pronoun, grammatically it must always be singular, but the word "they" is plural, which creates an error.) Answer (C), using all plural pronouns by changing "anybody else" to "other people," is the best answer to this problem.

51. **A**

Choice (A) is logical, smooth, and clear. Choice (B) is unclear because the *-ing* phrase is in the wrong place. Choice (C) seems to say that the writer explains how things work by remembering them, which is not what the original sentence means. Choice (D) repeats the word *things* twice, and is less direct than (A).

52. **B**

Choice (A) has an unclear pronoun reference—*they*. Choice (C) has a misplaced prepositional phrase that makes the meaning unclear. Choice (D) has a misplaced relative clause that seems to imply that the telescope was built by Martians.

53. **B**

Competition provides parallel structure with the other nouns in the sentence—*changes* and *factors*. Choices (A) and (C) are not nouns. Choice (D) is a gerund (an *-ing* word used as a noun), but it would only be parallel if used with other gerunds.

54. **A**

Dramatically means *drastically* or *in a major way*, and it tells the reader why the dinosaurs had problems with the changes. Choice (B) may be true but does not describe in what way their world was changed. Choices (C) and (D) imply that the dinosaurs were able to appreciate the *mystery* or the *thrill*, which is not supported by the article.

55. **C**

The specific "trouble" the asteroid caused was the *destruction* of much of the dinosaur's habitat and therefore of life as it then existed on earth. *Danger* (A) is only a potential problem, and the terms *worry* (B) and *hassle* (D) are too general and not nearly strong enough to describe the terrible events that will occur if an asteroid hits the earth.

56. **C**

The first part of the sentence is active voice, so we can eliminate (A). The placement of the word *even* in (B) changes the meaning of the sentence. Choice (D), Leave as is, uses a different pattern than the first part of the sentence. Choice (C) is the best because it is active voice and follows the same pattern as the first part of the sentence.

57. **D**

Choice (A), *so*, needs a second part (...*so important that*...). Choice (B), *that*, is also not correct by itself. Choice (C) is exaggerated. Choice (D), *very*, is the best choice for this sentence.

58. **A**

Important is an adjective that is often followed by an infinitive (*to* plus the simple form of the verb). Choice (B) is also an infinitive but in the passive voice, which should not be used unless there is a good reason. Choice (C) would be fine if the article dealt with the past. Choice (D) is an incorrect combination of an infinitive and a gerund.

59. **D**

This sentence is an example of a preposition (*to*) used with a gerund, or in this case, two gerunds. Choices (A), (B), and (C) are not parallel and can be quickly disregarded.

60. **D**

The poem does not specifically identify the object she is holding, but there are clues in the context. First, "a basket of the finest shells" is near her. Second, there is "an ocean cave within." It would be illogical to think that there is an actual ocean cave in something small enough that she can hold it up to look at it, so it is important to imagine something small that contains something that seems like a cave. There is nothing to indicate that Choice (A) is possible, and it does not fit in with the context of the seashore. Choices (B) and (C) cannot be "held aloft."

61. **A** ————————————————————————————

Light and brightness are often used to symbolize happiness. Choice (B) might seem correct at first glance, because "bright" can mean intelligent. However, the context of the stanza also mentions her laughter, so intelligence would not relate well with the poem. Choice (C) could also seem correct in a different context, but this poem has nothing to do with popularity. Choice (D) could reflect the bright future of youth, but again, the context of the stanza indicates otherwise.

62. **A** ————————————————————————————

A short piece of writing with this type of rhythm and imagery would need to be either a song or a poem. Essays (B), short stories (C), and plays (D) are all longer, less rhythmic, and less densely packed with imagery.

63. **A** ————————————————————————————

A comma is required after a subordinate clause at the beginning of a sentence (unless the sentence is very short). Choice (B) puts the comma after the verb, but it needs to go at the end of the clause. Choice (C) puts the comma after the first word of the main clause, between the subject and the verb—also incorrect. Choice (D) has no comma at all.

64. **A** ————————————————————————————

This sentence follows the same rule as number 63: The comma must go at the end of the initial subordinate clause. Choice (B) ignores the comma rule, and Choice (C) is in the present tense, which contradicts the rest of the sentence. The original sentence has an extra comma after the subordinating conjunction (D).

65. **D**

This is another example of parallel structure. The original sentence contains a series of three gerund phrases. Choices (A), (B), and (C) are each examples of faulty parallel structure: The three things they have in a series are not all the same type of words or phrases.

66. **C**

This question is about correct placement of the words "(while...) riding a bicycle." Wrong placement gives the sentence the wrong meaning. Choices (A), (B), and (D) imply that the dog was riding the bicycle.

67. **A**

Choice (B) has a sentence fragment and can immediately be rejected. Choice (C) uses an unusual and strange-sounding word order. Choice (D) is grammatically correct and the meaning is clear, but it uses the passive voice, and is not as clear or direct as Choice (A).

68. **B**

The best choice is (B), a complete sentence that describes one man's poetry in the present tense. Choice (A) is grammatically correct but the use of the future (will) gives it the wrong meaning. Choices (C) and (D) use an *-ing* verb form that cannot stand alone as the complete verb of a sentence.

69. **D**

To *proceed* means to continue with a planned activity and is the correct choice here. Choice (A) is not a correct verb form to use after the modal verb *should*. Choice (B) means "to come before." *Precedent*, (C), is not a verb at all.

70. **C**

Adjectives with more than two syllables form the superlative by adding the word *most*. *More beautiful* (B) is a comparative adjective, and this sentence is not comparing but rather singling out one "super" example. Choice (A) is an incorrect form and is not a real English word, and Choice (D) is the wrong meaning.

71. **C**

To join two clauses (SVs) we need either a period, a semicolon, a colon with a capital letter, or a correctly punctuated connector. Choice (A) does not capitalize the first word of the second clause after the colon. Choice (B) uses only a comma, which is not strong enough to connect two independent clauses in English. Choice (D) uses a connector but does not punctuate it correctly.

72. **B**

This is another example of a superlative adjective. One-syllable adjectives form the superlative by adding -*est*, although sometimes spelling rules apply. Choices (A), (C), and (D) are all incorrect forms.

Writing Task Sample Essays

On the following pages are example essays with scores that would have been given for the writing task. For Scoring Guidelines, please see the "Response to Writing Prompt" score guide in the Appendix. (Used by permission.)

"Response to Writing Prompt—Informational Essay"

4 Score Point 4
Student Response *

Commentary

While thinking about a moment in history that has influenced our world today, many events come to mind. But an event that seems prominent is not an event at all, but rather a time period and the accomplishments that took place within it, the Industrial Revolution.

Having learned about the industrial era just recently a few aspects remain vivid in my mind, such as the many new inventions that served to make our lives easier. The steam engine was developed allowing cities to form in locations other than near water sources, as things has been previously. Once inside those cities, people all came together working in factories which was much more efficient.

Through the factory system, goods were produced at a much faster rate, requiring less work so prices were less. Different social classes could afford items causing a change in social structure. Women and children began working stirring up awareness and laws about labor. Unions were formed as a result as well as more organized forms of education. Every aspect

In this 4 response, the writer addresses all parts of the writing task, which is to discuss a moment in history and share its importance in the world today. The writer provides a meaningful thesis that suggests that the events that took place during the Industrial Revolution have influenced our world today. This is followed with purposefully organized support to illustrate just why this period in history was so influential.

In the second paragraph, the writer discusses how the steam engine positively affected the growth of cities and how factories grew in the cities.

An additional discussion on the factory system is developed in the third paragraph. The writer provides thoughtful support through the use of specific details to illustrate the effects that factories had on people. More detail is included to show how the existence of factories helped create unions, causing a "change in social structure."

As the essay comes to a close, the writer provides more detail about the Industrial Revolution to connect its positive effect on how it "brought us to the way our world is today."

* The student response has been typed as written, with the student's own content, grammar, spelling, and punctuation.

Note: Sample student essays and commentary are reprinted, by permission, from California High School Exit Exam (CAHSEE), California Department of Education, P.O. Box 271, Sacramento, CA 95812-0271.

of life changed within this time period including advances in medicine, communications, and the way we manufacture today. The moments throughout the Industrial Revolution hold so much importance, they brought us to the way our world is today.

The variety of sentence types and the use of precise, descriptive language all add to the success of this essay. There are only a few errors of the conventions of written English within this response, and they are generally first-draft in nature. Overall, this essay is a sample of a 4-point response.

3 Score Point 3
   Student Response *

Commentary

One of the most important days in history so far is the day that man set foot on the moon. This was not only important in U.S. history, but it was important to everywhere else in the world too. This amazing achievement showed Americans that they can do anything they want, if they try hard enough, and it showed other countries how great we really are.

The day that man set foot on the moon was a very exciting day. A lot of people didn't believe that it really happened because it was so amazing. But when everyone realized that it really happened, it gave them the courage to strive for their goals and achieve them.

For years before man stepped on the moon, other countries had been trying to and were unsuccessful. But, America was able to. This made the other countries have so much respect for us.

Today's space missions can be traced directly to the success of the moon landing. When man set foot on the moon, it was honestly one of the most important days in history because of what took place as a result of it.

In this 3 response to the writing prompt, the writer discusses "…the day that man set foot on the moon." The thesis expresses the idea that this event was an amazing achievement that affected both Americans and the rest of the world and that it proved that "…Americans can do anything they want, if they try hard enough…"

The thesis is supported in an organized manner with details and examples. In the second paragraph, the writer concludes that the event was responsible for giving people "…the courage to strive for their goals and to achieve them." In the third paragraph, the writer suggests that other countries respect the United States for having walked on the moon.

The writer concludes with the idea that setting foot on the moon was "…one of the most important days in history…"

The writer addresses all parts of the task through discussion on what the event was and how it affected the world today. The details and examples used to support the thesis are more general than in a 4 response, but they do successfully support the thesis.

The use of a variety of sentences along with a general sense of audience is evident throughout the essay. There are a few errors in the conventions of English language, but they do not interfere with the reader's understanding of the essay. Overall, this essay is a sample of a 3 response.

---

* The student response has been typed as written, with the student's own content, grammar, spelling, and punctuation.

2   **Score Point 2**
Student Response *

Commentary

A moment in history that I has studied was when Ben Franklin discovered electricity. Electricity is important today, we use it for a lot of stuff. If he did not discover electricity, we probably wouldn't have a lot of stuff that we have now like lights, heat, air conditioning and a lot other things. He could have gotten electrocuted trying to discover it. So it is a good thing that he had find it out. Without electricity we can' do a lot of stuff we do now. We would have to use candles for light or just day light.

Within this 2 response to the writing prompt, the writer discusses Ben Franklin's discovery in a very limited manner. No explanation is provided on the event itself. The writer only provides few details to support the idea that "electricity is important today..." Through the use of basic, predictable language, the idea that "...we probably wouldn't have a lot of stuff that we have now" is suggested. The language used to support this idea is limited to the word "stuff" that appears three times in this very short paragraph.

There is very little variety at the sentence level and there are several errors in the conventions of the English language. The overall word choice and lack of development illustrate a very limited sense of audience. This essay exemplifies all the criteria within a 2 response.

* The student response has been typed as written, with the student's own content, grammar, spelling, and punctuation.

1   Score Point 1
   Student Response *

Commentary

We studied about all kind of stuff in History. Everything we stuyed in History I learned Something know everyday. History is go because you get to learn about all kinds of knew things abouat whats going on In this world.

In this 1 response, the writer provides no thesis related to the prompt beyond the idea that "we studied all kind of stuff in History." No attempt is made to discuss an event in history.

The ideas presented are no more than a brief discussion on the value of learning history. They are expressed through a lack of control at both the sentence and the language level. There are errors in the conventions of written English in each of the three sentences written in this 1 response.

* The student response has been typed as written, with the student's own content, grammar, spelling, and punctuation.

CAHSEE
English-Language Arts

Practice Test 2

Practice Test 2

Read the following document and answer questions 1 through 5.

HOW TO CHOOSE A PASSWORD*

Passwords are commonly used today to restrict access to personal possessions or privileged information. Passwords consist of a unique sequence of characters—letters, numbers, and symbols—required to access personal banking information, automated teller machines, secure buildings and businesses, computer networks, certain Web sites, e-mail, and more. Passwords are much like keys. Each password is different, and only the correct one allows the right of entry. It should be something unusual enough that the wrong person could not decipher it just by knowing you.

Before you can choose a password, however, you must know the types of passwords required. First find out if all letters must be lowercase or if upper- and lowercase are both acceptable. Should the password consist of letters or numbers only, or are special characters permissible? What is the minimum and maximum length allowed?

Note: Readings marked with an asterisk (*) are reprinted, by permission, from *California High School Exit Exam (CAHSEE)*, California Department of Education, P.O. Box 271, Sacramento, CA 95812-0271.

Now you are ready to think of an appropriate password. Your password should be something you can easily remember but something impossible for anyone else to decode or guess. We will discuss poor options first, so you will know what to avoid. Poor choices include names of people, family or fictional characters, common sequences such as QWERTY on the keyboard or 789456123 on the numeric keypad, or *any* word that appears in a dictionary. Other inappropriate choices include your telephone number or birth date. Do not use your middle name, mother's maiden name, your street name, or any other familiar name or number in reverse order.

The best way to choose a password that is hard to crack, yet easy to remember, is to select something memorable from your past. It could be the name of your grandparents' dog when you were 5 (*tippy5*) or the name of your math teacher in room 118 (*118-Thompson*). You could form a string of characters using the first letter of each word in a phrase or saying that makes sense to you. For example, your mother might say, "The sun is shining—So am I." A password derived from this saying might be (*TsisSaI*) or (*Tsis-SaI*).

Once you have created a good password, keep it safe. Do not store it in a computer or leave a handwritten copy where others might see it. You could put the number in your address book in a disguised form. It is not likely that anyone who found Ted Williams, 35 N. Sheldon Ave. in your address book would know it contains your password (TW35NSA).

It is best to have different passwords for each system. If you have used the same password for your bike lock and your access code to the Internet, would you be willing to loan your bike and lock to a schoolmate?

Since unauthorized access to sensitive information could open the door for an unscrupulous individual to access or even tamper with your personal records, as well as those of other people on the system, it is wise to change your passwords frequently. Some authorities suggest changing passwords every three months.

Bad Passwords:		Good Passwords:	
782-8973	(phone number)	**NYTXvincent**	(best friend in first grade preceded by state of birth and current state of residence)
Butch	(nickname)		
LittleBoPeep	(storybook character)		
12-11-86	(birth date)	**delygd**	(first letters of coach's favorite saying: Don't ever let your guard down.)
dejavu	(foreign phrase)		
leahcim	(name spelled backwards)	**ofcmgr98**	(mother's abbreviated job title—Office Manager—in 1998)
QQQQQQ	(repeated letter)		
XyzXyzXyz	(repeated pattern of letters)		

1. **Based on information in the document, which statement about passwords is accurate?**

   A   Computer programs cannot be protected by passwords.

   B   Passwords may not be used as a security measure in the future.

   C   People only need to use one password for different systems.

   D   Bad passwords could give access to unauthorized individuals.

2. **Which sentence from the document BEST summarizes the author's main point?**

   A   It is best to have different passwords for each system.

   B   Before you can choose a password, however, you must know the prerequisites for the password.

   C   Your password should be something you can easily remember but something impossible for anyone else to decode or guess.

   D   Some authorities suggest changing passwords every three months.

3. **What suggestion does the article provide about writing down passwords?**

   A   Write it down often so you don't forget your password.

   B   Disguise your password when you write it down.

   C   Do not let people know your password.

   D   Change your password frequently when you write it down.

4. **Based on information in the two boxes at the end of the document, *lkjlkj* would be a bad choice for a password because it—**

   A   is someone's initials.

   B   stands for a favorite saying.

   C   is a repeated pattern of letters.

   D   is an abbreviation of a familiar name.

5. **The key points of this paper are presented in the following order:**

   A   Definition of password, Password security, Types of passwords, Passwords to avoid

   B   Types of passwords, Password security, Passwords to avoid, Definition of password

   C   Password security, Definition of password, Passwords to avoid, Types of passwords

   D   Definition of password, Types of passwords, Passwords to avoid, Password security

The following is a selection from an employee manual explaining the job description of working at a video rental store. Read the article and answer questions 6 through 10.

Main Street Movies Employee Manual: Organizing Videos*

In order to help customers find what they want quickly and to keep track of inventory, it's important to keep the thousands of titles in the Main Street Movies store organized properly. This section of the *Employee Manual* will tell you how to organize videos so that customers will always be able to find them. It will also help you familiarize yourself with the store layout, so that you can help a customer find a particular film or a particular genre of film.

Each Main Street Movies store has three main sections:

1. New Releases Wall

2. Film Library

3. Video Games

New Releases Wall. Almost 70 percent of movie rentals are new releases, and that is the first place that most customers go when they enter the store. The center section of shelves on this wall holds **Hottest Hits**. When new titles come into the store (about 40 per month), place them on this wall in alphabetical order.

After 30 days, move the Hottest Hits titles to the shelves on either side, again in alphabetical order. The shelves flanking Hottest Hits are called **Recent Releases**. Titles stay on the Recent Releases shelves eight to ten months before being moved to Film Library shelves. The New Releases Wall, including the Hottest Hits and Recent Releases shelves, holds about 350 titles.

Film Library. The thousands of titles in the Film Library are organized into categories (genres). The films within each category are displayed alphabetically. Here are the categories and their two-letter computer codes:

AC	Action	FA	Family	SC	Science Fiction
CH	Children	FL	Foreign Language*	SI	Special Interest
CL	Classics	FO	Foreign	WE	Western
CO	Comedy	HO	Horror		
DR	Drama	MU	Music		

*Foreign Language titles include films that were originally made in a foreign language, films that have been dubbed into a foreign language, and films with foreign language subtitles. A sticker on the back of each box specifies which type of film it is.

Special Interest includes these sub-categories:

AN	Animation	IN	Instruction	SP	Sports
DO	Documentaries	RE	Religion	TR	Travel
EX	Exercise				

Video Games. Main Street Movies carries games for Super Nintendo, Sony Play Station, and Nintendo 64 game systems. Games for all three systems are arranged together, in alphabetical order.

Although video games represent only a small percentage of our inventory, they are shoplifted more often than any other type of merchandise in our store. Therefore, video games are *never* displayed on the shelves. Shelves in the Video Game section of Main Street Movies hold cardboard plaques with pictures and information about each game. When a customer wants to rent a particular game, he or she will bring you the plaque. You then retrieve the game from the locked case behind the counter, rent it to the customer, and file the cardboard plaque in the "Video Game Rentals" box. When the game is returned, put the plaque back on the appropriate shelf so that it is available for another customer.

6. **What is the order in which new movies are moved through the store?**

   A from Hottest Hits to Film Library to Recent Releases

   B from Film Library to Hottest Hits to Recent Releases

   C from Hottest Hits to Recent Releases to Film Library

   D from Recent Releases to Film Library to Hottest Hits

7. **Which of the following is NOT a subcategory of Special Interest?**

   A animation

   B exercise

   C religion

   D western

8. **A customer wants to know if a Foreign Language video has subtitles. Based upon the manual, what is the best way to find this information?**

   A Look at the back of the box.

   B Check the computer.

   C Ask an employee.

   D Watch a few minutes of the film.

9. **About what percentage of movie rentals are from the Film Library?**

   A 100%

   B 70%

   C 30%

   D This information cannot be determined from this reading.

10. **Which of the following categories has the newest videos?**

    A Recent Releases

    B Film Library

    C Special Interest

    D Hottest Hits

The following articles discuss the opposite viewpoints of using vitamin supplements. Read both articles and answer questions 11 through 16.

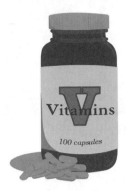

PRO AND CON ON VITAMIN SUPPLEMENTS*

Pro: The Key to a Long and Healthy Life

No medical breakthrough means so much, to so many people, as the discovery of the role of nutrition in human health and longevity. Numerous scientific studies have shown that specific nutrients hold the key to a strong heart and cardiovascular system, a healthy immune system, a normal nervous system, and more. They can help prevent cancer, loss of memory and vision, physical and mental defects in newborns, and degeneration of health in seniors. Vitamins and minerals are essential to the healthy function of every system within our bodies; without them we would not have the energy to perform even the simplest daily task. Perhaps the most important part of any healthy diet, therefore, is a nutritional supplement. The simple "vitamin"—a comprehensive formula of high-quality, high-potency vitamins and minerals—is a sure source of nutrition that can lead to better health, a longer life, and a better quality of life for years to come.

Those who recommend against a daily supplement, relying on a balanced diet instead, are unrealistic and uninformed. Few people consume the right amounts or types of foods to meet the recommended daily intake of vitamins and minerals. To get a full day's supply of calcium, for example, you'd have to consume 1 cup of milk, PLUS 1 cup of chopped broccoli, PLUS one cup of navy beans, PLUS one cup of plain yogurt, PLUS four ounces of canned pink salmon.

The U.S. Department of Agriculture's (USDA's) Food Guide Pyramid recommends eating 2-3 servings each of meats and dairy products, 2-4 servings of fruits, 3-5 servings of vegetables, and 6-11 servings of breads, cereals, rice, and other grains every day. Most people don't meet those guidelines. Some groups in particular, such as senior citizens, find it hard to squeeze that many servings into their daily diets. In a special food guide pyramid modified to address the needs of older Americans, the Tufts University USDA Human

Nutrition Research Center specifically recommends supplements of calcium, vitamin D, and vitamin B12— vitamins many older adults find difficult to get in adequate amounts from food alone.

Even people who get the recommended number of servings may not get the nutrition they expect. In this world of fast and processed food, little nutritive value is left in the food we eat. On top of that, many essential nutrients, such as vitamin C and the energy-producing B vitamins, are water-soluble. Because they are not stored in the body, adequate amounts must be consumed every single day. A supplement is like nutritional insurance. It fills the nutritional gap between the foods you eat and the amount you need. But even if you could meet the recommended daily values for every nutrient every day, would that be enough for vibrant good health? Probably not. Scientific studies show that some vitamins and minerals can fight the aging process and strengthen your immune system—but only at levels far higher than the recommended daily value. Only through supplementation can you regularly and reliably get the high potencies needed for optimal good health.

Today, good nutrition is as close as the grocery store shelf. Help yourself to a daily vitamin and mineral supplement, and help yourself to improved health and longevity.

Con: Danger in Disguise

Today, we know that the role of vitamins and minerals goes well beyond the prevention of deficiency diseases, such as scurvy, to actually preventing cancer and heart disease, the most fearsome and ferocious killers of our time. With this knowledge has come the widespread call for nutritional supplementation—and a confusing array of vitamin, mineral, and herbal supplements lining the supermarket shelves.

Far from contributing to better health, however, nutritional supplements threaten to turn a scientific breakthrough into a nutritional disaster.

Promoters of vitamins and minerals—especially the antioxidant vitamins A, C, and E—would have consumers believe that the little vitamin pill in the bottle is all they need for good health. Take your vitamins in the morning, and you're covered. It's okay to eat fast food for the rest of the day or skip meals to achieve today's fashionably skinny look. But vitamins and minerals are only one part of the nutritional puzzle. A diet rich in fiber and balanced in carbohydrates and protein is essential for good health. You can't get these things from a nutritional supplement. The focus on vitamin and mineral supplements may actually be robbing us of the full nutrition we seek.

And no supplement can compare to the quality of nutrition found in natural sources. For example, our bodies convert carotenes from plant foods into vitamin A. Many supplements contain a single carotene, beta-carotene. Natural sources are rich in many different carotenes, many of which are much more potent antioxidants than beta-carotene. Many supplements contain a synthetic form of vitamin E, when natural vitamin E is more readily absorbed and used by the body. And science is still discovering the wealth of nutrients in foods, including oligomeric proanthocyanidins (OPCs) found in grapes. These antioxidants are up to 50 times more powerful than vitamin E and are efficiently used by the body.

You'd be hard-pressed to find a supplement as nutritionally comprehensive and potent as a balanced diet. Even if you could, you'd pay much more than if you got the same nutritional value from natural sources.

But perhaps the greatest danger presented by nutritional supplements comes from the very real risks presented by self-medication. Anyone can walk into the market and buy as many different supplements as desired. The reported benefits of high dosages of certain nutrients have led some people to believe that the more the better. Many take several vitamin and mineral supplements without regard to total intake or possible interactions.

High-dose supplements of vitamin A can cause toxicity, leading to bone fractures, joint pain, liver failure, and other significant symptoms. Excess vitamin D can result in kidney damage. Too much vitamin K can interfere with anti-clotting medications. Because these fat-soluble vitamins can be stored in the body, where excess amounts can build up to dangerous levels, experts recommend supplementation only with a doctor's supervision.

Surprising new research suggests that vitamin C pills may speed up hardening of the arteries, the underlying cause of heart attacks and strokes. Researchers said their findings support the recommendations of health organizations, which urge people to avoid high doses of supplements and to get their nutrients from food instead.

As appealing as they're made to sound, nutritional supplements are danger in disguise. If you're looking for good health, don't look on the supplement shelves of your supermarket. Look in the produce section instead.

11. **Read this sentence from the first article.**

> A supplement is like nutritional insurance.

What does the author mean by comparing the use of supplements to insurance?

A   Like nutritional supplements, insurance is necessary in order to maintain good health.

B   Having insurance and using supplements will keep bad health away.

C   Both insurance and vitamins are important in curing health problems.

D   Like insurance, the nutritional value of supplements will be available when you need it.

12. **Read this sentence from the first article.**

> Help yourself to a daily vitamin and mineral supplement, and help yourself to improved health and longevity.

What does the sentence mean?

A   Helping others means encouraging them to take vitamins and minerals.

B   A large helping of vitamins and minerals is necessary for good health.

C   Taking vitamins and minerals is one way that people may help themselves.

D   Taking vitamins and minerals regularly will have a positive effect on a person's health.

13. **Instead of depending heavily on vitamin supplements, the author of the second article encourages readers to—**

A   eat fruits and vegetables.

B   begin an exercise program.

C   skip meals when necessary.

D   limit the intake of protein.

14. **What information supports the idea that vitamin supplements are potentially dangerous?**

A   Supplements are usually available in powder, tablet, and liquid form.

B   People might accidentally take supplements that interfere with medications.

C   Supplements may play a large role in disease prevention.

D   People tend to be too cautious when using supplements.

15. **Based on the second article, which of these statements is true?**

A   Vitamin supplements provide adequate carotenes for the human body.

B   A mineral supplement may be as full of nutrients as a balanced diet.

C   Vitamin supplements are less valuable than eating a variety of healthy foods.

D   A surplus of vitamin supplements can be beneficial to some people.

16. **Read the following phrase from the reading:**

> ...a strong heart and
> cardiovascular system...

What does "cardiovascular" mean?

A   related to a balanced diet

B   related to vitamin and mineral supplements

C   related to the heart and pumping of blood

D   related to the body's system of fighting disease

The following story is about the author's love for "going home." Read the story and answer questions 17 through 21.

Going Home*

Some days, I go to school, and on the way to school, I think that there is nowhere else in the world I would rather be. No matter what time of year it is, I walk through the neighborhoods, and every morning, I see the same people I always see: the tiny old lady walking what may be the tiniest dog in the world, the man at the newsstand with the walrus mustache, the skipping twins on their way to the bus stop. I don't know any of their names or where they live, or what their favorite foods are, or what they think about anything, but these are people I've known forever. In a strange way, I think of them as my friends. Every day, I smile at them, and they smile at me. The man at the newsstand says "Buenos días" in his deep voice and will sometimes comment on the weather in Spanish because years and years ago I told him that my parents spoke Spanish too, and he told me I needed to learn. When it rains, the old lady with the dog always scolds me and tells me I should carry an umbrella.

And school—it's the same. What I like best is the routine: homeroom, English, biology, physical education, lunch, math, and social studies, then soccer practice after school. I see the same people at school every day, sit next to the same people in my classes, eat lunch with my same friends. I have friends I have known as long as I can remember. It's as comfortable as being at home.

My parents moved into our house before I was born. I know everything there is to know about our street. The oak tree in the yard has a tree house that my father built when I was six. The sidewalk is cracked in front of our neighbors' house from the big earthquake; we use the uneven pavement as a skate ramp. If you run past the tall fence in front of the big white house on the corner, you can see through the fence as if it didn't exist.

At breakfast my parents give each other a look, and I know something is going to happen. Before they can say anything, I want to know what it is all about.

"Nothing bad," my father says.

I look at my mother, and she gives me a smile of reassurance and pats my shoulder. "You should be happy, Carlos. This is only good news." What I see on their faces is worry.

"We're going to move," my father says.

Today on my way to school I look at everything as if seeing it for the first time. The tiny old lady waves at me; her tiny dog wags its tail and gives a tiny bark. The man at the newsstand greets me. The skipping twins almost run me off the sidewalk, but they veer in the other direction and race off to the bus stop. I feel like a different person, a stranger, someone who really might be seeing these people for the first time. No longer are they the familiar landmarks of my daily trek to school. After I move with my family, I might never see them again, and I am filled with an indefinable feeling. I don't know if it's loneliness or grief.

For the first time ever, my school day is not comfortable. All day long, I feel constricted and restrained, the way you feel when it's winter and you're wearing layers of sweaters under your jacket, and everything feels too tight and you can't move. My English teacher's voice sounds high-pitched and scratchy; my friends say the same things they always do, but today it seems boring; my lunch tastes like chalk; and my pitches in P.E. class go wild, as if they have a mind of their own. In social studies, the teacher lectures from the chapter we read the night before, so it's like knowing how the movie ends before you sit down in the theater. Going home from this day is a relief—until I remember that we're moving.

I try to imagine living somewhere else, but all I can see is a blank space, a question mark, an empty page. All I know is my life. All I know is where I live, where I go, what I do here. I have been other places—I have visited my grandparents in Texas and my cousins in Mexico, and once we took a trip to New York. You can visit anywhere, but until you walk the same route to school every day for years, what do you know? You can know about the average rainfall and the geographical landmarks, but where is the best place to get a milkshake?

My mother comes up to my room and tells me that my father has gotten a promotion. That's why we are moving.'"Don't you want to know where we're going?" she asks.

"Not really," I say. She tells me anyway. I pretend not to listen.

Every day, my parents tell me something about the town that will become our new home. There is a bronze statue honoring World War II veterans in the park downtown. In the summer, there are rodeos at the county fair. There is an annual strawberry festival. The mayor used to be a pro football player. There are oak trees in our new neighborhood, just like the one in our yard.

Images of oak trees and rodeo clowns and strawberries and statues begin to fill in the blank space in my mind. I start wondering what it might be like to live in this town where the mayor presides at all the high school football games, and the strawberries are supposed to be the best in the world.

On the day before we move, I walk in the same direction as I would if I were going to school. When I see the tiny old lady, I tell her good-bye, and she tells me to carry an umbrella when it rains. Her tiny dog holds out a tiny paw to shake my hand. The man at the newsstand shakes my hand, too. The twins wave as they board the bus. I go home, walking slowly through streets lined with oak trees.

A huge truck is parked in front of our house. The movers are carrying boxes while my parents are loading suitcases into our car. Soon our house will be empty. But not for long; I know that somewhere there are parents telling their children about a town filled with oak trees, a place where you can get the best milkshake in the world, a place where, if you're lucky, you might see the same people every day of your life.

17. **Why does the narrator take a walk on the day before the family moves?**

   A to take one last look at everything familiar

   B to visit the statue in the middle of town

   C to see if the same people are still in the same places

   D to be away from home when the movers come

18. **Read this sentence from the selection.**

   > … I know that somewhere there are parents telling their children about a town filled with oak trees, a place where you can get the best milkshake in the world…

   What makes the preceding statement ironic?

   A the fact that, like the narrator, other children are worried about moving

   B the fact that, like the people in the narrator's neighborhood, most people enjoy their homes

   C the fact that, like the narrator's father, parents often get promotions

   D the fact that, like the narrator's home, every house has its stories

19. **What does the author emphasize by having the narrator see the same people three different times in the story?**

   A that the narrator feels at home in this town because nothing ever changes

   B that the narrator's life is repetitive and boring because nothing ever changes

   C that the new town the family is moving to will have similar people to meet

   D that the new children who move to the narrator's house will become comfortable in it

20. **Which line from the story indicates the writer's heritage?**

   A I see the same people at school every day

   B There are oak trees in our new neighborhood

   C In a strange way, I think of all of them as friends

   D I have visited my grandparents in Texas and my cousins in Mexico

21. **Based on the information in the story, what is the narrator's mood?**

   A sad, curious, and a little worried

   B happy, excited, and curious

   C grouchy, angry, and nervous

   D nostalgic, comfortable, and relaxed

The following story is about a character who discovers a book of quotations in the library. Read the story and answer questions 22 through 29.

A Word in the Hand*

It might have been destiny that left Marco waiting in the library for his sister. Whatever it was, Marco waited impatiently, tapping his fingers on the table until a librarian gave him a warning glance. He tapped his foot until the librarian sent another cautionary glance his way. Marco stood up, stretched, yawned, and viewed the stacks of books, the shelves of books, the books in every direction, books as far as the eye could see. He picked one randomly off the shelf: *Everyday Quotations and Proverbs*. Marco thumbed through the pages, a little bored. To be honest, Marco wasn't much of a reader. He didn't mind reading, but it just wasn't his favorite thing to do.

A line caught his eye. It was a quotation he had heard before, a million times at least, something his mom said to him all the time. This quotation was from the sixteenth century, was over 400 years old, and was still kicking around today. Marco read on. The more he read, the more he found that sounded familiar. He moved a stack of magazines off a chair and sat down, still reading. He found a saying to fit every situation and every occasion. There were proverbs that offered instruction on everything, from loaning money to friends (not a good idea, according to the wisdom of the ages) to making excuses. Marco kept reading.

When his sister finally showed up, Marco didn't even notice. Alicia practically had to shout to get him to look up. Then she was the one who had to wait, somewhat impatiently, while Marco applied for and received a library card so he could check out the book and take it home.

"Come on," said Alicia. "Hurry up. Mom said to make sure we got home in time for dinner."

"Haste makes waste," said Marco calmly as he got into the car and put the key in the ignition.

"What's wrong with you?" Alicia wanted to know.

Marco pointed to the book that lay on the console between them. "Knowledge is power."

"You're crazy," she said.

"Birds of a feather flock together."

"Whatever. All I know is that if we're late for dinner, Mom's going to be mad."

"A soft answer turns away wrath."

Alicia's only response was to gape at Marco, her mouth slightly open.

Marco himself was surprised by the proverbs popping out of his mouth. The sayings had taken on a life of their own.

At dinner, Marco declined a serving of green beans.

"Marco, you need to eat some vegetables," said his mother.

"Waste not, want not," Marco replied.

When Marco's mother asked him what was new, Marco shrugged and said that there was nothing new under the sun. When Marco's father said that he had hired a new assistant, Marco nodded in approval and said that a new broom swept clean and that two heads were better than one. When his mother said that she had gotten stuck in the development phase of a new project,

Marco said sympathetically, "Back to the drawing board." As an afterthought, he cautioned that if she wanted anything done right, she would have to do it herself. Alicia mentioned that she had snagged her favorite sweater on the sharp corner of a desk. Marco told her there was no use in crying over spilt milk. Alicia looked at him as if she had never seen him before. "Be quiet, please." Her tone was anything but polite.

"It takes two to make a quarrel," Marco instructed her.

"I guess it only takes one to act like an idiot," his sister replied. "Stop it!"

"Familiarity breeds contempt," said Marco sadly. "Let's forgive and forget."

"Marco," his father said sternly, "discretion is the better part of valor."

"That's right," said his mother in her strictest voice. "Besides, this is all Greek to me!"

Both of his parents started laughing.

"Laughter is the best medicine," said Marco.

"Oh, well," said Alicia, relenting. "Better to be happy than wise."

"Good one," said Marco, surprised.

Alicia smiled. "If you can't beat them, join them."

22. Read this sentence from the selection.

> "Familiarity breeds contempt."

What does the word *contempt* mean in this sentence from the story?

A alarm

B dislike

C emotion

D confusion

23. How does Marco's family react to his use of proverbs?

A His parents are surprised; his sister is upset.

B His parents are irritated; his sister is impressed.

C His parents are entertained; his sister is annoyed.

D His parents are disturbed; his sister is encouraging.

24. What does Marco mean when he says to his sister, "Birds of a feather flock together"?

A If he is crazy, then she must be crazy, too.

B She must set a good example for him.

C She, not he, is the crazy one.

D If she plans to stay out of trouble, they must unite.

25. What did Marco mean in the following sentence from the story?

> Marco told her there was no use in crying over spilt milk.

A Marco wanted Alicia to feel OK about spilling the milk.

B Marco was warning Alicia to be careful with the milk.

C Marco thought Alicia should be sad about snagging her sweater.

D Marco wanted Alicia to feel OK about snagging her sweater.

26. What does the word "discretion" mean in the following sentence from the reading?

> "Marco," his father said sternly, "discretion is the better part of valor."

A spending money however seems right

B knowing when to stop

C teaching something new

D learning something new

27. **Which line from the reading foreshadows the main events of the story?**

    A   It might have been destiny that left Marco waiting in the library for his sister.

    B   He didn't mind reading, but it just wasn't his favorite thing to do.

    C   He found a saying to fit every situation and every occasion.

    D   "If you can't beat them, join them."

28. **What is the meaning of "gape" in the following sentence from the story?**

    > Alicia's only response was to gape at Marco, her mouth slightly open.

    A   wonder

    B   stare

    C   yell

    D   frown

29. **Which of the following phrases from the story is an example of an idiomatic expression?**

    A   "waited impatiently"

    B   "was surprised"

    C   "asked him"

    D   "showed up"

Read the following poem and answer questions 30 through 34.

I've Watched ...*

I've watched the white clouds pantomime
The inner workings of my mind,
Where thought and feeling paint a scene
As if the blue sky were a dream.

5   I've watched the snow-bogged trees bend down
And shake their coats upon the ground
In order that they may reclaim
A straighter truth from whence they came.

I've watched the congress of the geese
10 Assemble in a perfect V
In order that they may keep sight
Of one another's path of flight.

I've watched the flood tide turn its head
And slack before the coming ebb
15 Without want or predilection
Waiting for the moon's direction.

I've watched the ocean lashed by wind,
Make a fool of the fishermen,
Who thought their knowledge of the sea
20 Ensured them some security.

But all this watching, knows not much,
For what are wind and sea and such,
The V of geese, the bent-down tree,
If nothing more than mystery?

30. **Which phrase BEST represents the organization of the poem?**

    A   5 stanzas about nature and 1 about people

    B   5 stanzas of observation and 1 of conclusion

    C   1 stanza of introduction and 5 of explanation

    D   1 stanza about poetry and 5 about nature

31.

> I've watched the ocean lashed by wind

In this line from the poem, the word *lashed* suggests that the ocean is being—

    A   soothed.

    B   troubled.

    C   sailed.

    D   whipped.

32. **According to lines 17–20, the fishermen's knowledge of the sea—**

    A   reflects their love of natural elements.

    B   helps them navigate more effectively.

    C   is greater than their knowledge of the weather.

    D   does not guarantee them safety.

33. **What is the theme of the poem?**

    A   Clouds can be a reflection of our thoughts.

    B   Geese assemble in the shape of a V to navigate properly.

    C   Nature remains a mystery, regardless of our observations.

    D   Trees often bend beneath the weight of the snow.

34. **Which of the following lines from the poem includes an example of personification (the use of personal characteristics to describe something that is not actually a person)?**

    A   The inner workings of my mind

    B   As if the blue sky were a dream

    C   Assemble in a perfect V

    D   I've watched the flood tide turn its head

The following story describes a young boy's heroic actions to help his injured brother. Read the story and answer questions 35 through 39. The writing task on page 329 also refers back to this story.

Hiking Trip*

"I never wanted to come on this stupid old hiking trip anyway!" His voice echoed, shrill and panicked, across the narrow canyon. His father stopped, chest heaving with the effort of the climb, and turned to look at the boy.

"This is hard on you, son, I know. But you've got to come through with courage and a level head."

"But I'm scared! I don't even want to have courage!" he retorted. He jerked his head the other way and wiped his eyes across his arm.

"If not courage, fine," his father replied sternly. "Then have enough love for your brother to think this through!" He pulled a bandana from his back pocket and tied it around his neck. Then he gently placed his hand on the boy's shoulder and continued, more softly this time. "Now, I don't know if I can make it without stopping every so often. And we just don't have the time to stop. You're young, but you're strong and fast. Do you remember the way back from here to the road, if you had to go alone?"

Jeff flashed back to the agonizing scene of his seventeen-year-old brother at their campsite that morning. He'd been bitten by a snake yesterday during a rough hike through very rocky terrain. By the time they returned to their tents, he was limping badly. Then this morning he couldn't put on his boots, and the pain seemed to be getting worse. He needed medical attention right away, so leaving him there was their only choice.

"Jeffrey? Jeffrey, could you do it? Could you make it to the road without me if you had to?"

Jeff blinked and looked past his father's eyes to the end of the canyon, several miles away. He nodded slowly as the path and the plan began to take hold in his mind. "What was the name of that little town we stopped in to get matches, Dad?"

His father smiled and replied, "Flint. After we left Flint, we parked at the side of the road a few miles out of town. When you see which way our car is facing, you'll know that the town is back the other direction." Jeff thought about this and then nodded. They both drank water and then continued scrambling over the rocks.

Nothing was as pretty as it had seemed when they first hiked this way to their campsite. Before, the boulders and rocks had been an interesting challenge. Now, they were obstacles that threatened their footing and their velocity. Overhanging limbs had earlier been natural curiosities in the cliffs. But now they were nature's weapons, slapping and scratching the boy and the man who crashed by and pushed through as quickly as they could.

Stone by stone, they made their way up the canyon. Jeff's father grew smaller and smaller in the distance. "He must be stopping a lot," Jeff thought. He waved to him from a bend in the canyon wall. His father waved back. Jeff turned and made the final ascent up an easier slope toward the road and spotted his father's car. He lurched toward it, half stumbling, and leaned on the hood, breathless.

"Can't stop," he thought. "Mark's in big trouble. Gotta keep going." The fast, loud thudding in his ears was deafening, and as he pulled himself upright, he was surprised as a car sped by, heading toward Flint. "Hey, mister!" he shouted, waving both arms. He began to walk, faster and faster until he was jogging. Then he quickly crossed the highway and broke into a full-speed run, holding his left arm straight out, his thumb up.

His chest was burning with every breath when he suddenly heard several loud honks from behind. He turned as the brakes squealed and saw "Bob's Towing & Repair, Flint" right behind him. "Jump in, boy! What's up?" Jeff explained between gasps as the truck picked up speed. The driver reached for his two-way radio as soon as he heard about Mark. "Better get the helicopter in there," he seemed to be shouting into his hand. But Jeff wasn't sure about that because everything got fuzzy and then went black and quiet.

Hours later, Jeff opened his eyes to find strange surroundings and his father on a chair nearby.

"You're a hero, son," his father said with a smile. "You saved Mark."

"What happened?" Jeff asked through a wide yawn. "Where are we?"

"This is a motel room in Flint. You made it into town and sent the helicopter into the canyon after Mark. I can't tell you how happy I was when I saw it overhead. I'm so proud of you!"

Jeff sat up suddenly. "Where's Mark? Is he OK?"

"They airlifted him out and got him to the hospital. His leg's still in bad shape, but he's going to be just fine in a couple of days. Thanks to you, son."

Jeff's worried face relaxed as his father spoke. "How about you, Dad? How did you get out?"

"Well, I finally hiked myself out of that canyon and to the road. I won't be going back there any time soon. That's for sure. Anyway, I couldn't see the car, and as I headed for Flint I got lucky and was able to hitch a ride from a fellow named Bob in a tow truck."

Jeff laughed out loud. "I guess Bob makes a good living going up and down that road. I hope you gave him a good tip, Dad!"

35. **This story is an example of which of the following genres of writing?**

A a narrative short story

B an informational text

C a persuasive essay

D a biographical essay

36. **Which of the following sentences BEST explains Jeff's biggest problem in the story?**

A He needed to face his fear of losing his father's respect.

B He needed to find someone to take him to the town of Flint.

C He needed to climb the rock-covered hill to get to the top.

D He needed to face his fear in order to help his brother.

37. **What kind of person is Jeff's father in the story?**

A understanding and motivating

B aggressive and annoying

C humorous and entertaining

D impatient and anxious

38. **Read the following line from the story.**

> But Jeff wasn't sure about that because everything got fuzzy and then went black and quiet.

What happened to Jeff?

A He passed out.

B He went to bed.

C He rode in a helicopter.

D He was in the tow truck when it crashed.

39. **This short story includes which of the following forms of literature to communicate its meaning?**

A comedy

B poem

C drama

D dramatic monologue

The following short story describes the sensations and feelings the writer experiences as she swims a race. Read the story and answer questions 40 through 46.

The Race

It starts with a last call to the starting line. The timers signal ready, the whistle is blown, and the last thing I see is the person in the lane next to me turn her head and smile the instant before she jumps.

The shock of the cold hits me first, the slap of the water, the roar of the crowd. Now comes the easy part, the automatic part that kicks in as it has been so relentlessly programmed to, whenever my body comes in contact with water. My feet churn up a storm and my arms follow the path of the water that they have been forced to memorize for the past 10 years. My mind can rest now; I can enjoy the way the bottom of the pool looks so blue and clean through the goggles and be annoyed when they begin to slowly fill up with water and blur my once perfect vision. This is my thinking time, this is where I rest, this is who I am. My body won't fail me here, and I am….

Before I have a chance to finish the thought, the concrete side of the pool rushes out to meet me, and I am welcomed back to reality by the cheering crowd. Deliciously exhausted, which I didn't notice until now, I drag my body out of the pool and empty my goggles. I try to look surprised when they announce I've won. I attempt to be humble, modest, feign embarrassment, find a seat in the sun, and wait for my next race to be called.

It starts with a last call to the starting line.

40. **Which adjective best describes the swimmer's attitude?**

    A boredom with the routine

    B fear of losing

    C anger toward the other swimmers

    D pride in her abilities

41. **Why does the author refer to the crowd more than once?**

    A to give the impression of danger

    B because the swimmer feels lonely

    C to contrast the private thoughts of the swimmer with the public noise of the crowd

    D to show that the swimmer was the crowd's favorite

42. **How does the author feel about her swimming ability?**

    A surprised and humble

    B proud and happy

    C irritated and exhausted

    D modest and embarrassed

43. **Why does the author use the exact same words in the introduction as in the conclusion?**

    A to show that racing is important to the swimmer

    B to show that the swimmer is afraid that she will lose the next race

    C to show that the swimmer will have the same experience again

    D to show that the swimmer is reliving the race in her mind

44. **The words "relentlessly" and "forced" in the reading convey a feeling of _____.**

    A dedication

    B imprisonment

    C happiness

    D sadness

45. **The expression "deliciously exhausted" in the story gives it a _____ tone.**

    A competitive

    B satisfied

    C hopeless

    D ecstatic

46. **While swimming, the author experiences a sensation of _____.**

    A being in her own world

    B anger because her opponent smiled at her

    C concentrating on winning the race

    D sadness because she might not win

The following is a rough draft of an article explaining h_____rite an essay. It may contain errors in grammar, punctuation, sentence structure, and organization. Some of the questions may refer to underlined or numbered sentences or phrases within the text. Read the article and answer questions 47 through 51.

Essay Writing*

(1) To begin an essay, a student should have some knowledge of the topic or be willing to search out information. (2) Then <u>one</u> must focus clearly on the prompt, addressing all its major points, and making sure that the central purpose is evident throughout the entire essay. (3) Interesting and convincing examples with lots of specific details are always helpful. (4) The details must show some kind of clear arrangement—chronological, spatial, or order-of-importance. (5) A student writer will also want to revise a first draft <u>so that any errors in grammar and mechanics can be got rid of</u>. (6) Steps can be taken to edit essays. (7) Relying solely on "SpellCheck" can be risky; (8) it does not catch the common errors that students make, such as confusing "your" and "you're." (9) If students meet all these requirements, then they will have written very effectively.

47. Which of the following sentences, if inserted before sentence 1, would make the MOST effective opening sentence?

    A   Writing an essay is easy if one uses a computer.

    B   Good essays are always written in black pen.

    C   Any student can write a successful essay.

    D   Teachers sometimes assign difficult essays.

48. Which is the MOST effective substitution for the underlined part of sentence 5?

    A   and ridding of errors in grammar and mechanics.

    B   to get rid of errors in grammar and mechanics.

    C   and getting rid of errors in grammar and mechanics.

    D   Leave as is.

49. What is the best way to express the underlined word "one" in sentence 2?

    A   she

    B   he

    C   he or she

    D   Leave as is.

50. What is the best way to express the ideas in sentence 6?

    A   Steps to edit essays can be taken.

    B   To edit essays, steps can be taken.

    C   Students can take steps to edit essays.

    D   Leave as is.

51. What is the best way to express the ideas in sentence 9?

    A   If students meet all these requirements, then they had written very effectively.

    B   Students have been writing very effectively if they meet all these requirements.

    C   If students will have written very effectively, they meet all these requirements.

    D   Leave as is.

The following is a rough draft of an essay that discusses the legend of the Abominable Snowman. It may contain errors in grammar, punctuation, sentence structure, and organization. Some of the questions may refer to underlined or numbered sentences or phrases within the text. Read the essay and answer questions 52 through 55.

The Abominable Snowman*

(1) The Abominable Snowman is a hairy, apelike <u>thing</u> that is said to live in the Himalayan Mountains of Nepal. (2) Natives of this region have believed in the existence of this beast for many centuries. (3) However, since no one has ever found a Yeti (the Nepalese name for the Abominable Snowman), doubts still remain.

(4) Some people who believe in the Yeti point to the discovery of peculiar footprints found above the snowline of the Himalayas. (5) There were footprints left by animals, and some people think that they were very much like human footprints but that they must have been made by animals which were much heavier and larger than humans. (6) Scientists who have studied the footprints, however, agree that they were most likely left by bears. (7) "Bears are quite capable of walking on their two hind legs," says zoologist Hans Miller. (8) "This also explains many supposed Yeti sightings. (9) At a distance, a bear walking in such a way could easily appear to be a creature of human form. (10) In fact, three of the five Yeti sightings last year were determined to be bears. (11) The others remain unexplained." (12) Nonetheless, many people remain convinced that the Yeti is real. (13) "There has to," says Raju, a mountain guide, "be something out there. (14) There have been too many sightings for this all to be the product of overactive imaginations." (15) And, yet, it seems that the world will not be convinced of the existence of the Yeti until it is confirmed by hard evidence, a live specimen, or at least a skeleton. (16) For now, it appears that the Yeti will continue to inhabit the shadowy region between legend and reality.

52. Which of the following words is the BEST way to express the meaning of the word *thing* in sentence 1?

   A   object

   B   item

   C   creature

   D   article

53. Which of the following ideas is supported by details or evidence in the essay?

   A   The world will never believe in the existence of the Yeti.

   B   Yeti sightings cannot be explained by overactive imaginations.

   C   A bear walking on its hind legs can appear to be a Yeti.

   D   All mountain guides believe in the Yeti.

54. What is the BEST way to write sentence 13?

   A   "There has to be something out there," says Raju, a mountain guide.

   B   "There has to be something out there, says Raju, a mountain guide."

   C   "There has to, says Raju, a mountain guide, be something out there."

   D   Leave as is.

55. Based on the essay, which of the following would be the BEST source of information to demonstrate that the Yeti most likely does NOT exist?

   A   a book of Nepalese legends which contains stories about the Yeti

   B   a documentary about the Yeti containing interviews with Yeti believers

   C   a poster which has pictures of all known Himalayan mammals

   D   a magazine article which demonstrates the falsehood of all supposed Yeti sightings

The following is a rough draft of an essay in which the author discusses why many people are choosing to travel by train. It may contain errors in grammar, punctuation, sentence structure, and organization. Some of the questions may refer to numbered sentences or phrases within the text. Read the article and answer questions 56 through 59.

Traveling by Train*

(1) Traveling by train is becoming more and more popular. (2) Some people prefer to travel by plane. (3) There are many reasons why people are choosing to travel by train. (4) One reason is that trains are a more relaxing way to travel.

(5) When people ride a train, they don't have to stay seated during the entire trip. (6) They can get up and walk around and they can go to the restaurant car when they get hungry. (7) Some people like to go to the observation car where they can look at the view through many windows.

(8) Business people like to travel by train so they can work while they ride. (9) There are places with tables where people can set up their computers and work while they ride. (10) Even though it may be faster to travel by plane, many people are discovering the relaxing and often productive time on a train.

56. Which of the following sentences does NOT relate to the thesis of the essay?

A There are many reasons why people are choosing to travel by train.

B Business people like to travel by train so they can work while they ride.

C Some people prefer to travel by plane.

D One reason is that trains are a more relaxing way to travel.

57. Which of the following statements could be added to the essay to support the main idea?

A Trains have been around since the middle 1800s.

B Some trains even have ways to hook up computers to the internet.

C Most trains are very slow and cause people to become bored while traveling.

D There aren't enough trains to meet the needs of travelers.

58. Which of the following is a more effective way to express the ideas expressed in sentence (1)?

A More people are traveling by train today.

B Train travel is more popular now than before.

C Traveling by train is becoming increasingly more popular.

D More people travel by train than before in the past.

59. Which of the following resources would provide further information about train travel today?

A "Train Travel, the Modern Way to Go." Editorial. Los Angeles Times 17 Mar.

B Rouse, Thomas. The Invention of the Steam Engine. New York: Random, 1998

C Krauseburg, James. "Trains, Automobiles, and Airplanes: A Look at the History of Travel." Atlantic Monthly Jan. 1999: 33-34.

D Trains: Their Tie to America's Past. 20 Mar. 1995. U.S. Train Society. 25 Mar. 1999 <www.ustrain society.com>.

For questions 60 through 65, choose the answer that is the most effective substitute for each underlined part of the sentence. If no substitution is necessary, choose "Leave as is."

60. When our parents celebrate their silver wedding anniversary later this year, <u>they were married for twenty-five years</u>.

    A they will have been married for twenty-five years.

    B they have been married for twenty-five years.

    C they would have been married for twenty-five years.

    D Leave as is.

61. <u>Akia told us about her safari across the plains of East Africa in our geography class.</u>

    A In our geography class, Akia told us about her safari across the plains of East Africa.

    B Akia told us about her safari in our geography class across the plains of East Africa.

    C In our geography class Akia told about her safari across the plains of East Africa to us.

    D Leave as is.

62. <u>If Mark will have made fewer errors, he will have passed his driving test.</u>

    A If Mark would have made fewer errors, he would have passed his driving test.

    B If Mark had made fewer errors, he would have passed his driving test.

    C If Mark would of made fewer errors, he would have passed his driving test.

    D Leave as is.

63. <u>"Why should I wear a sweater?"</u> grumbled the boy as his mother reminded him again of the cold weather.

    A 'Why should I wear a sweater'?

    B "Why should I wear a sweater"

    C "Why should I wear a sweater"?

    D Leave as is.

64. The Alaskan rivers are clear and sparkling <u>in summer however, they are frozen in winter</u>.

    A in summer, however they are frozen in winter.

    B in summer; however, they are frozen in winter.

    C summer: however they are frozen in winter.

    D Leave as is.

65. What is the BEST way to express the following idea?

    My brothers share a room. <u>It is theirs room.</u>

    A It is my brothers room.

    B It is my brother's room.

    C It is my brothers' room.

    D Leave as is.

For questions 66 through 72, choose the best word or phrase to complete the sentence.

66. The musician played Wendy's favorite waltz for her husband and _____.

   A I

   B he

   C she

   D her

67. _____ going to be late if they don't hurry.

   A They're

   B Their

   C There

   D They'll

68. When she _____ the award, she blushed and quickly returned to her seat.

   A excepted

   B accepts

   C accepted

   D excepts

69. Mount Everest is _____ than all other mountain peaks.

   A more higher

   B higher

   C the highest

   D more high

70. Because fruits and vegetables are important parts of a healthy diet, _____.

   A so we need to eat a good variety of them.

   B we need to eat a good variety of them.

   C therefore, we need to eat a good variety of them.

   D for that reason, we need to eat a good variety of them.

71. Please bring the following materials to class with _____ books, pens and pencils, paper, and a calculator.

   A you:

   B you;

   C you

   D you…

72. The purpose of this demonstration is _____ and entertain.

   A instruction

   B instructing

   C instructional

   D to instruct

Writing Task:*

In the story "The Hiking Trip," which you read on pages 315–317, the reader learns about the main character, Jeff. Jeff's personality and emotions are revealed through the actions and dialog presented in the story.

Write an essay in which you describe the personality and emotions of Jeff, the main character. How do his personal characteristics add to the events in the story? How does the author reveal this information about Jeff in the story? Use details and examples from the story to support your ideas.

Checklist for Your Writing

The following checklist will help you do your best work. Make sure you:

- ❑ Carefully read the reading passage and the description of the task.

- ❑ Organize your writing with a strong introduction, body, and conclusion.

- ❑ Use specific details and examples from the passage to demonstrate your understanding of the main ideas and the author's purpose.

- ❑ Use precise language that is appropriate for your audience and purpose.

- ❑ Vary your sentences to make your writing interesting to read.

- ❑ Check for mistakes in grammar, spelling, punctuation, capitalization, and sentence formation.

STOP

Answer Key

1.	D		25.	D		49.	C
2.	C		26.	B		50.	C
3.	B		27.	C		51.	D
4.	C		28.	B		52.	C
5.	D		29.	D		53.	C
6.	C		30.	B		54.	A
7.	D		31.	D		55.	D
8.	A		32.	D		56.	C
9.	C		33.	C		57.	B
10.	D		34.	D		58.	C
11.	D		35.	A		59.	A
12.	D		36.	D		60.	A
13.	A		37.	A		61.	A
14.	B		38.	A		62.	B
15.	C		39.	C		63.	D
16.	C		40.	D		64.	B
17.	A		41.	C		65.	C
18.	A		42.	B		66.	D
19.	A		43.	C		67.	A
20.	D		44.	A		68.	C
21.	A		45.	B		69.	B
22.	B		46.	A		70.	B
23.	C		47.	C		71.	A
24.	A		48.	B		72.	D

Detailed Explanations of Answers

PRACTICE TEST 2

1. **D**

Choice (A) is the opposite of the main idea. Choice (B) is a true statement but not included in this document. The reading directly contradicts (C).

2. **C**

Choices (A), (B), and (D) are true but only give details, not the main idea. Only choice (C) reflects the idea indicated by the title, "How to Choose a Password."

3. **B**

This answer is directly stated in the reading. Choice (A) is not included in the reading at all. Choice (C) is in the reading, and it is good advice, but it does not answer this question. Choice (D) is a combination of two different ideas that do not appear together in the reading.

4.　Ⓒ ———————————————————————

The left-hand box contains a similar example of a bad password along with the explanation: "(repeated pattern of letters)." Choices (A) and (D) are also bad passwords, but they do not answer the question—neither one is mentioned in the box at the end of the reading. Choice (B) would be an example of a *good* password, according to the right-hand box, but the question asks for a *bad* choice. Be sure to read the headings of boxes and other similar parts of a reading.

5.　Ⓓ ———————————————————————

The very first paragraph of this reading contains a definition of a password, which eliminates answers (B) and (C). The first line of the second paragraph indicates that it is about different types of passwords, which eliminates (A).

6.　Ⓒ ———————————————————————

Skimming the first part of the reading will give you the information that Hottest Hits is the first place that videos go, eliminating (B) and (D). The next paragraph states that movies are moved to Recent Releases after 30 days, eliminating (A).

7.　Ⓓ ———————————————————————

Skimming for the words "Special Interest" will bring you to the second box, which includes all of the above choices except *Western*. Another way to find this would be to see that in the first box, *Western* is listed as a major category, not a sub-category.

8. **A**

This information is located in the footnote with an asterisk (*) below the first box. By skimming for *Foreign Language* and noticing the asterisk, you can find the information quickly. Choices (B) and (C) may or may not find you the information, but they are not included in the manual. Choice (D) is definitely a way to find out if it has sub-titles, but again, the question asks "Based upon the manual...."

9. **C**

The reading states that "almost 70 percent of movie rentals" are new releases. By subtracting 70 percent (B) from 100 percent (A), you will soon find that about 30% of the videos are from the Film Library. Choice (D) is incorrect because even though the information is not directly stated in the reading, it can be inferred.

10. **D**

Recent Releases (A) includes all of the newest movies, but also the ones that have been there over 30 days. Choice (D) is a better answer because Hottest Hits includes only the newest videos. Choice (B) contains videos that have been on the shelves for over eight months. Choice (C) is a category within the Film Library.

11. **D**

This statement from the reading requires some analysis to decide what the best answer is. Insurance is something you may or may not need, but it's good to have just in case you need it. In the same way, the author is saying that vitamin supplements are good to have in case you don't get enough nutrients from your food. Choices (A), (B), and (C) are not directly stated or even implied in the reading.

12. **D**

The best paraphrase of this sentence includes the same main points. These are: 1) taking vitamins and minerals, and 2) improving health. Choice (A) and (C) do not mention improving health, and Choice (B) adds information that is not in the sentence.

13. **A**

The "con" article mentions "plant foods," "natural sources," and "foods." Choices (B), (C), and (D) are not mentioned in the reading—they are just common sense.

14. **B**

"Interfering with medications" is definitely a potentially dangerous situation. Choices (A) and (D) are neither beneficial nor dangerous. Choice (C) is beneficial.

15. **C**

The main points of the second article are that 1) vitamin supplements are not as good as eating a variety of foods, and 2) overuse of vitamin supplements is potentially dangerous. Choices (A), (B), and (D) are the opposite of these points.

16. **C**

There are two ways to find the meaning of "cardiovascular." The first way is from the root word "cardio-." "Cardio" exercise means exercise that raises the heart rate. "Cardiac care" means taking care of people who have heart problems. A "cardiac arrest" is a heart attack.

The second way is to pay attention to the *context*, which includes a list of body systems. "Cardiovascular" is referred to together with "heart," so even if you don't know the meaning, you can probably guess that it is related to "heart," so (C) is the best answer.

17. **A**

The second paragraph from the end of the reading tells us that the narrator takes a walk and says good-bye to the people he usually sees every day. Even though it is not stated directly, we can infer that he wants to see them one more time before he moves. The fact that he walks slowly indicates that he wants to enjoy the moment. Choices (B), (C), and (D) are not supported by the reading.

18. **A**

The ironic thing about the narrator's thoughts is that other children are moving to the town he is leaving, and their parents are telling them about it so that they won't worry either. Choices (B), (C), and (D) do not relate to this sentence.

19. **A**

Repetition is a strategy that writers use to emphasize something, and in this case, it implies that everything the narrator sees in his neighborhood is always the same. The tone of the narrator's interactions with these people is comfortable rather than boring, so (A) is a better answer than (B). Choices (C) and (D) may be true statements, but they are not supported by this experience.

20. **D**

Heritage refers to people's background, such as their religion and ethnicity, location where they grow up, and even what family they are a part of. Choices (A), (B), and (C) do not mention any of these points.

21. **A**

The word "mood" refers to the feelings of the narrator (the person who is telling the story.) The narrator is the boy whose family is getting ready to move. Even though he is curious about his new home, he is not happy or excited, so (B) is not correct. He is probably nervous and possibly a little grouchy, but there is nothing in the story to indicate that he is angry, so (C) is not correct. He is definitely nostalgic, but not really comfortable and relaxed, because he is not sure what his new home will be like, so (D) is also incorrect. Choice (A) is the only answer that is completely correct.

22. **B**

One good strategy is to substitute each of the choices for the word *contempt*. By doing this you should find that Choices (A), (C), and (D) do not accurately reflect what happened in the story.

23. **C**

The story includes many clues that his sister is either upset (A) or annoyed (C), including "anything but polite" and "'Stop it!'". This eliminates (B) and (D). Alicia and Marco himself are surprised at his new habit, but there is nothing in the text to indicate that his parents are surprised. Finally, his parents started laughing, which leads us to believe that they are entertained.

24. **A**

This proverb means that the same kind of people usually spend time together. Therefore, if she says that he is crazy, then she must be crazy too. Choices (B), (C), and (D) do not reflect the correct meaning of this proverb.

25. **D**

The sentence before this one in the story talks about Alicia snagging her sweater. This proverb means that what happened in the past is over, so there is no use becoming too worked up about it. There is no milk in the story, which eliminates (A) and (B). Choice (D) makes more sense in this context than (C).

26. **B**

Discretion means good judgment, whether with money or in another situation. Because Alicia is annoyed by Marco's continual use of proverbs and sayings, (B) is the best answer. Money (A) is not mentioned in the story, and Choices (C) and (D) are not related to the situation in the story.

27. **C**

To *foreshadow* is to provide a preview of some sort of what will happen later in a reading. The main events of this story relate to Marco's use of proverbs and sayings in every situation, so (C) is the best answer. Choice (A) does foreshadow something, but it does not mention the main events of the story. Choice (B) is just a detail. Choice (D) is just an example of a saying.

28. **B**

"Gape" and "gaping" can be learned from vocabulary study or from extensive reading. If you have never read these words before, try to expand both the types and amounts of material you read. Answer (A) refers to Alicia's thoughts, and not to the facial expression indicated. "Yell" (C) does not fit the story, and "frown" (D) has a completely different meaning. (B) is the only correct answer because it means to *stare with extreme surprise, usually with the mouth open.*

29. **D**

An idiomatic expression is a group of words that means something different when used together from what the individual words seem to indicate. Answers (A), (B), and (C) mean literally what they say, so they are not idiomatic expressions. The expression "showed up" does not mean to *show* anyone anything, or to raise anything *up* in any way. It is an idiomatic expression that means "to arrive."

30. **B**

The first four stanzas are observations of nature, and the fifth stanza is an observation of both nature and people. The final stanza is a conclusion. Choice (A) is close, but not quite accurate. Choice (C) is not correct because the first stanza is about observing nature and there is no introduction, and there is no stanza about poetry (D).

31. **D**

To *lash* means to hit, especially with a whip of some sort. Soothed (A) means *calmed*, the opposite of the meaning of this line of poetry. Choice (B), *troubled*, is not as strong as lashed, and *sailed* (C) has a completely different and unrelated meaning from *lashed*.

32. **D**

The observation "make a fool of the fishermen" suggests that they are not in control of their boats on the windy ocean. This helps us to eliminate (A), (B), and (C), which all have positive connotations of the fishermen's situation. By a process of elimination, the best answer is the one with a negative connotation: (D).

33. **C**

The *theme* is the most important idea or feeling communicated by the poem. Answers (A), (C), and (D) are in the poem as specific examples, but only (C) is supported by all the other parts of the poem. The theme is often found at the beginning, or, as in this case, at the end of a reading.

34. D

The flood tide is not a living creature, but it is described as turning its head. Choice (A) refers to an actual person. Choices (B) and (C) do not assign personal characteristics at all.

35. A

A narrative short story tells what happens with a main character who has at least one obstacle to overcome. This reading is obviously not just to provide information (B). It does not try to persuade the reader of anything (C), and it does not explain how a person is by telling stories about his or her life (D).

36. D

The first paragraph of the story indicates that Jeff felt panic (was scared). The reason he needed to overcome his fear was so that he could get help for his brother. Choice (A) might be true, but the story doesn't indicate it, and in any case it could not possibly be as urgent as getting help. Choice (B) is true, but it is not the BEST answer. (It is very important to read each question carefully.) Choice (C) is not true—there is a narrow canyon and rocky terrain, but no rock-covered hill.

37. A

Words used to describe Jeff's father include *stern*, *gently*, and *softly*, and he indicates that he understands how Jeff is feeling. He keeps urging and asking Jeff to do what he needs to do to save his brother. Choices (B) and (C) are not mentioned in the story at all. The father may or may not be impatient and anxious (D) because of the dangerous situation, but the story doesn't show that he is.

38. A

To *pass out* means to lose consciousness, which is what happened to Jeff. He was in a truck, not a bed (B). His brother was airlifted out, but Jeff didn't ride in the helicopter (C), and the tow truck didn't crash (D).

39. C

The serious events of the story make this a drama rather than a comedy (A). It is not in the form of a poem (B), and more than one person speaks, so it cannot be (D).

40. D

There are several clues in the last part of the reading that tell us that the swimmer is proud of herself. There is nothing to indicate that the swimmer is bored (A), afraid (B), or angry (C).

41. C

The swimmer hears the crowd both at the beginning and end of her race, when its noise welcomes her back from her private underwater world. There is a thrill, but no danger (A), and nothing in the reading indicates that either (B) or (D) is true.

42. B

The author pretends to feel surprised, humble (A), modest, and embarrassed (D). She is happy (deliciously exhausted) rather than irritated (C).

43. **C**

Choices (A), (B), and (D) may or may not be true, but the introduction is what starts the race, and by repeating it at the end of the short story, we can infer that the experience will soon be repeated.

44. **A**

Relentlessly and *forced* refer to the physical and mental training the swimmer has forced herself to complete. They could also refer to (B) or (D) in a different context, but there is nothing in this story to support either interpretation. Choice (C) conveys a completely different meaning.

45. **B**

This question requires a knowledge of the connotations (shades of meaning) of these words. "Deliciously exhausted" gives the feeling of being tired but in a satisfactory way. Choice (A) is not directly related to being exhausted after the race. *Hopeless* (C) would contradict *deliciously*, and *ecstatic* (D) has a much stronger meaning or connotation.

46. **A**

The author's statements "This is my thinking time..." and "...back to reality..." indicate that, while she is swimming, she feels apart and separate from the rest of the world. There is no indication that she is angry (B) or sad (D), and instead of concentrating (C), she is experiencing "the easy part, the automatic part...."

47. **C**

This rough draft of an article is missing a topic sentence, which needs to include the main idea of the essay—writing a successful essay. Choices (A) and (B) might be good points to include in the body of the paper, and Choice (D) is too general to be the topic sentence.

48. **B**

"to get rid of errors..." uses an infinitive to show the purpose, which fits well into this sentence. Choices (A) and (C) are not grammatical, and the existing wording is passive voice, extremely informal, and does not represent standard American usage (D).

49. **C**

Choices (A) and (B) would imply that the article only applies to one gender of student. The use of "one" (D) does not refer back directly to "a student," and it is also a very formal usage in a paper that is somewhat relaxed and informal in tone.

50. **C**

Choice (C), in the active voice, is direct and to the point. The other three choices, (A), (B), and (D), are all in the passive voice, which in this case does not serve a useful purpose and should therefore be avoided.

51. **D**

Although Choice (D) is not the only correct way to express this idea, it is the best option given. Choices (A) and (B) are in past time rather than the future, and Choice (C) is incorrect because the future perfect tense is used in an *if*-clause.

52. **C**

Creature is the only word that specifically refers to a living being. The other answers, (A), (B), and (D), generally refer to non-living objects and are very general.

53. **C**

Sentences (7), (8), (9), and (10) refer to evidence that supports answer (C). The words *never* (A) and *all* (D) make these choices incorrect. Choice (B) is a matter of opinion and not supported by the article.

54. **A**

This sentence is clearer if the quotation is not interrupted. Choice (B) puts the quotation mark in the wrong place, and Choices (C) and (D) interrupt the quotation.

55. **D**

Choices (A) and (B) would tend to support that the Yeti might in fact exist. Choice (C) does not prove anything except that the Yeti is not known to the makers of the poster.

56. **C**

By reading this question carefully, you will notice that it asks which sentence does NOT relate to the thesis of the essay. The thesis (main idea) of this essay is in sentence (1): "Travel by train is becoming more and more popular." Choices (A), (B), and (D) all support this point, leaving Choice (C) by process of elimination.

57. **B**

An Internet connection definitely makes trains more convenient. Choice (A) might be good background information but does not support the main idea. Choice (C) contradicts the main idea rather than supporting it, and Choice (D) may or may not be relevant to the main idea, because it could show increased demand for trains, or be an inducement *not* to take the train.

58. **C**

"Increasingly more popular" means the same thing as the original, "more and more popular." Choices (A), (B), and (D) miss the point that train travel is continuing to increase in popularity.

59. **A**

Only (A) provides more information about train travel today. Answers (B), (C), and (D) refer to trains in the past but not the present.

60. **A**

The future perfect tense (A) indicates an activity that takes place before another event in the future, so it is the best answer. Choice (B) is the present perfect tense, which indicates an activity that takes place before the present time. Choice (C) uses *would*, which makes the sentence conditional rather than factual. Choice (D) uses the simple past tense, not appropriate for a future event.

61. **A**

Place and time are often placed at the beginning of a sentence, and this placement contributes to a clear understanding of the meaning of this sentence. Choice (B) implies that the safari was in the geography class, and that the class was in East Africa. Choice (C) places the indirect object "us" in the wrong position and is not correct usage. Although place and time may also be placed at the end of a sentence (D), in this case it would seem to imply that East Africa was in the geography class.

62. **B**

In a subordinate clause such as an *if*-clause, the present tense is used to refer to future time. Choice (A) might sound all right, but the use of *would* in the if-clause makes this answer an incorrect one.

Choice (C) contains an incorrect spelling of *would've* (would of). Choice (D) uses the helping verb *will* in a subordinate clause, a violation of the grammar rules.

63.   D

A question is being quoted, so the question mark belongs inside of the quotation marks. Choice (A) uses single quotation marks, which is only for a quote inside of a quote. Choices (B) and (C) do not include the question mark inside of the quotation marks.

64.   B

Coordinating conjunctions such as *however* (when it connects two clauses) must be preceded by a period or a semicolon and followed by a comma. Choice (A) does not have a comma, Choice (C) uses a colon and also has no comma, and Choice (D) does not have a semicolon or a period before *however*.

65.   C

Since both brothers share a room, the apostrophe that shows possession must follow the word *brothers* and not *brother*, and brothers ends with an *-s*, so no additional *-s* is needed. Choice (A) does not show possession. Choice (B) means that the room is only inhabited by one brother, and *theirs* is a possessive pronoun being incorrectly used as an adjective in (D).

66.   D

The easiest way to find the answer to this question is to repeat the question without the other person: "The musician played Wendy's favorite waltz for _____." By trying each answer in the blank, you can quickly determine that (A), (B), and (C) are incorrect. The grammatical reason is that the first three answers are subject pronouns, but in this sentence we need an object pronoun.

67. **A**

This is an example of a question about commonly confused words. *They're* is the contraction of *they are*, which is correct in this sentence. *Their* (B) means *belonging to them*, *there* (C) means *in that location*, and (D) would be incorrect grammar in this sentence.

68. **C**

This is another commonly confused word. Choice (C) has the correct meaning (*to receive*) and is used in the past tense, which matches the rest of the sentence. Choices (B) and (D) are the wrong tense, and Choices (A) and (D) are forms of the wrong word, which means *to make an exception of*.

69. **B**

We need a comparative adjective here because of the word *than*. With few exceptions, one-syllable adjectives such as *high* form the comparative by adding *-er*. Choice (A) is a double comparative, which is not correct in modern English. Choice (C) is a superlative adjective, which doesn't work with *than*. Choice (D) is not the best method of forming the comparative form of a one-syllable adjective.

70. **B**

Choice (B) provides a main clause to go with the subordinate clause that begins with *because*. The other choices, (A), (C), and (D), all add an extra connector (*so*, *therefore*, and *for that reason*), which is incorrect. Sentences with two clauses only need one connector.

71. **A**

A colon (A) is used to introduce a list after a sentence that is already complete. In this situation, a semicolon (B), an ellipsis (D), or no punctuation at all (C) are all incorrect.

72. **D**

This is an example of the infinitive of purpose (*to* plus the simple form of the verb). The word *to* serves for both simple verb forms: *instruct* and *entertain*. Choices (A), (B), and (C) are not parallel.

Writing Task Sample Essays

On the following pages are example essays with scores that would have been given for the writing task. For Scoring Guidelines, please see the "Response to Literary/Expository Text" score guide in the Appendix. (Used by permission.)

"Response to Literature"

4   Score Point 4
Student Response *

     In the story "The Hiking Trip" Jeff had to hike down a canyon and go get help for his brother Mark. Jeff is courageous and loving, and his true character is revealed by his actions.

     The author gradually reveals Jeff's bravery through his actions and his decision to save Mark. At first, Jeff is afraid of hiking down the canyon alone. The father tells Jeff to have courage and Jeff exclaims that he doesn't want it. The father also tells Jeff to have enough love for his brother to save him. Even though he is afraid and doesn't want to hike down the canyon, Jeff does it anyways. He does it to try to save his brother. This point in the story shows Jeff's love for his brother and his determination to save him.

     This is the turning point in the story. If Jeff had not made the decision to hike down the canyon alone the outcome of the story may be entirely different. Jeff's bravery, love, and perserverance played an enormous role in this story. Without them he may have never tried or been able to save Mark.

Commentary

     In this response, the writer addresses all parts of the writing task, which include describing Jeff's personality and emotions, identifying the way the author reveals Jeff's personality, and relating Jeff's personality to the plot. The response also illustrates a comprehensive grasp of the text.

     The first paragraph of the response summarizes the main action of the story and states the thesis, that Jeff is courageous and loving and that his "true character is revealed by his actions."

     Next, the writer gives more detail about the main action of the story, using evidence from the text to show how Jeff's actions reveal his courage and love. Specific references to the text are included (e.g., "the father also tells Jeff to have enough love for his brother to save him").

     In the third paragraph, the writer focuses on the relationship between Jeff's personality and the plot, identifying the turning point in the story as Jeff's decision to go for help alone and tying this decision to Jeff's love and determination: "Without them he may have never tried or been able to save Mark."

* The student response has been typed as written, with the student's own content, grammar, spelling, and punctuation.

Note: Sample student essays and commentary are reprinted, by permission, from California High School Exit Exam (CAHSEE), California Department of Education, P.O. Box 271, Sacramento, CA 95812-0271.

This story shows how someone can overcome their own fears to help others. Jeff was an example of unselfishness, bravery, and courage. His character traits caused him to do what was right and they (his character traits) may have been the deciding point of his action and later on the outcomes of his story.

The use of precise language and a variety of sentence types add to the success of this essay. There are only a few errors in the conventions of written English within this response, and they are generally first-draft in nature. Overall, this essay is a sample of a 4-point response.

3

Score Point 3
Student Response *

Commentary

To understand who Jeff is, you have to realize what he has to go through in the story. In the beginning, Jeff is afraid to hike and doesn't want to have the courage to climb the mountain. After Jeff's dad says, "If not courage, fine. Then have enough love for your brother," Jeff realizes that he has to do it to save his brother's life. He becomes determined to find help. He thinks about how badly his brother needs medical attention.

Jeff becomes so determined to get help, he begins to climb faster and faster until he passes up his dad. He says to himself "Can't stop, Mark's in big trouble." This shows how his love for his brother has substituted for the courage that he did want to have. Do you think that his love for his brother gives him the courage or the will to climb the mountain and get help for Mark.

Hours later after Mark is rescued, Jeff wakes up but doesn't know what had happened. His father tells him that he's a hero and that he saved his brothers life. He had pushed himself to the limits trying to get help for Mark. His love for Mark had given him the will, the determination, and the courage to get over his fear and climb the mountain for help.

In this response, the writer explicitly or implicitly addresses all parts of the writing task and shows a good grasp of the text.

The first paragraph of the response summarizes the main action of the story and suggests the thesis that is later expressed in the final paragraph—that Jeff has determination, courage, and love. The second paragraph summarizes events in the story to show that the author uses the events to reveal Jeff's character, although this connection is not explicitly stated. The final paragraph sums up Jeff's role in the plot: "His father tells him that he's a hero and that he saved his brothers life." Again, this relationship is not explicitly stated.

The response represents a 3-point paper because it addresses all parts of the writing task and shows a good grasp of the story. Also, it makes specific references to the text (e.g., "Can't stop, Mark's in big trouble"). However, it lacks the purposeful control of organization and explicit statement of ideas that characterize a 4-point paper. The observations about Jeff's personality are structured by the story line rather than directed by the writer. The paper also illustrates an inconsistent sense of audience, as shown by the direct address to the reader in the first and second paragraphs.

There are only a few errors in the conventions of written English within this response, but they do not interfere with the meaning. Overall, this essay is a sample of a 3-point response.

---

* The student response has been typed as written, with the student's own content, grammar, spelling, and punctuation.

2   Score Point 2
Student Response *

Jeff, the main character shows much of his personality and emotions. He is an understanding and motivating person. He knows what strength he has but he doesn't know how to use it. Although Jeff has many fears and knows he must overcome them to save his brother. His father knows his sons power, but its Jeff who doesn't realize his own. Jeff doesn't have self confidence of self will. His emotions in the story change. He starts off as a boy who doesn't believe in himself, to a boy who's emotions completely change under the circumstances. He must save his brother in order know if he really has inner power inside of him. This was the test. His personal characteristics add to the event of the story by making it more intense. The more intense the better the story, He adds problem to the story line and a resolution He doubts his own strength but he ends up winning.

Commentary

In this response, the writer addresses some parts of the writing task and demonstrates a limited understanding of the main elements of the story. The response begins with three very general statements about Jeff's personality. Then the writer begins to focus on a potential thesis that could be supported by textual evidence: "Although Jeff has many fears and knows he must overcome them to save his brother." This statement also shows the writer's grasp of important ideas within the text. As the response continues, the statement that Jeff must overcome his fears receives additional development with the assertion that Jeff's emotions "completely change under the circumstances." However, these ideas receive no additional development through the use of textual evidence.

The final sentences of the response begin to address the relationship between Jeff's personality and the plot: "His personal characteristics add to the event of the story by making it more intense." One of these sentences uses the vocabulary of plot analysis ("He adds problem to the story line and a resolution") but provides little actual analysis.

The lack of a clear thesis statement and the failure to develop ideas by using evidence from the text are characteristic of a 2-point paper. The response also fails to demonstrate a purposeful control over organization. There is some variety in sentence structure, but there are several errors in the conventions of written English. Overall, this essay is an example of a 2-point response.

* The student response has been typed as written, with the student's own content, grammar, spelling, and punctuation.

1   **Score Point 1**
     Student Response *

Commentary

This story tells about a boy who has doesn't want to go on a trip with his father and learn more about hiking but then, when he gets their he realizes the important thing that is about hiking. His father was really understanding and motovating, one of the things Jeff new it was important to learn hiking was for what happened to his father the accident he had, he knew it was important cause he know what to do during an accident.

This response begins to address the writing task in its opening statement: "This story tells about a boy who has doesn't want to go on a trip with his father." However, there is little understanding of the main elements of the story; the response continues by implying that the primary issue is the value of hiking and that Jeff's father (not his brother) has had an accident.

The failure to demonstrate a grasp of the text, the lack of a main idea, the failure to develop ideas using evidence from the text, and the serious errors in the conventions of written English make this a 1-point response.

* The student response has been typed as written, with the student's own content, grammar, spelling, and punctuation.

Appendix:

CAHSEE Scoring Guides

Response to Literary/Expository Text

4 | **The response–**
- demonstrates a *thoughtful,* comprehensive grasp of the text.
- accurately and coherently provides *specific* textual details and examples to support the thesis and main ideas.
- demonstrates a *clear* understanding of the ambiguities, nuances, and complexities of the text.
- provides a *variety* of sentence types and uses *precise, descriptive* language.
- contains *few, if any, errors* in the conventions of the English language. (Errors are generally first-draft in nature.)*

Response to informational passages:
- *thoughtfully* anticipates and addresses the reader's potential misunderstandings, biases, and expectations.

Response to literary passages:
- clearly demonstrates an awareness of the author's use of literary and/or stylistic devices.

3 | **The response–**
- demonstrates a comprehensive grasp of the text.
- accurately and coherently provides *general* textual details and examples to support the thesis and main ideas.
- demonstrates a *general* understanding of the ambiguities, nuances, and complexities of the text.
- provides a *variety* of sentence types and uses *some descriptive* language.
- may contain *some errors* in the conventions of the English language. (Errors do not interfere with the reader's understanding of the essay.)*

Response to informational passages:
- anticipates and addresses the reader's potential misunderstandings, biases, and expectations.

Response to literary passages:
- demonstrates an awareness of the author's use of literary and/or stylistic devices.

2 | **The response–**
- demonstrates a *limited* grasp of the text.
- provides *few, if any,* textual details and examples to support the thesis and main ideas.
- demonstrates *limited, or no* understanding of the ambiguities, nuances, and complexities of the text.
- provides *few, if any,* types of sentences and uses *basic, predictable* language
- may contain *several errors* in the conventions of the English language. (Errors may interfere with the reader's understanding of the essay.)*

Response to informational passages:
- *may* address the reader's potential misunderstandings, biases, and expectations, but in a limited manner.

Response to literary passages:
- *may* demonstrate an awareness of the author's use of literary and/or stylistic devices.

1 | **The response–**
- demonstrates *little, if any,* comprehensive grasp of the text.
- may provide **no** textual details and examples to support the thesis and main ideas.
- may demonstrate **no** understanding of the ambiguities, nuances, and complexities of the text.
- may provide **no** sentence variety and uses *limited* vocabulary.
- may contain *serious errors* in the conventions of the English language. (Errors interfere with the reader's understanding of the essay.)*

Response to informational passages:
- does **not** address the reader's potential misunderstandings, biases, and expectations.

Response to literary passages:
- does **not** demonstrate awareness of the author's use of literary and/or stylistic devices.

non-scorable

B = Blank	**T** = Off-Topic
L = Written in a language other than English	**I** = Illegible / Unintelligible

* *Conventions of the English language refer to grammar, punctuation, spelling, capitalization, and usage.*

Note: Scoring Guides are reprinted, by permission, from *California High School Exit Exam (CAHSEE)*, California Department of Education, P.O. Box 271, Sacramento, CA 95812-0271.

Response to Writing Prompt

4

The essay –
- *clearly* addresses all parts of the writing task.
- provides a *meaningful* thesis, demonstrates a consistent tone and focus, and illustrates a *purposeful* control of organization.
- *thoughtfully* supports the thesis and main ideas with *specific* details and examples.
- provides a variety of sentence types and uses *precise, descriptive* language.
- demonstrates a *clear* sense of audience.
- contains *few, if any, errors* in the conventions of the English language. (Errors are generally first-draft in nature.)*

A Persuasive Composition:
- states and maintains a position, *authoritatively* defends that position with precise and relevant *evidence* and *convincingly* addresses the reader's concerns, biases, and expectations.

3

The essay –
- addresses all parts of the writing task.
- provides a thesis, demonstrates a consistent tone and focus, and illustrates a control of organization.
- supports the thesis and main ideas with details and examples.
- provides a *variety* of sentence types and uses *some descriptive* language.
- demonstrates a *general* sense of audience.
- may contain *some errors* in the conventions of the English language. (Errors do ***not*** interfere with reader's understanding of the essay.)*

A Persuasive Composition:
- states and maintains a position, *generally* defends that position with precise and relevant evidence and addresses the reader's concerns, biases, and expectations.

2

The essay –
- addresses *only parts* of the writing task.
- *may* provide a thesis, demonstrates an *inconsistent* tone and focus and illustrates *little, if any*, control of organization.
- *may* support the thesis and main ideas with *limited, if any*, details and/or examples.
- provides *few, if any*, types of sentence types, and *basic, predictable* language.
- demonstrates *little* or ***no*** sense of audience.
- may contain *several errors* in the conventions of the English language. (Errors **may** interfere with the reader's understanding of the essay.)*

A Persuasive Composition:
- defends a position with *little* evidence and *may* address the reader's concerns, biases, and expectations.

1

The essay may be too short to evaluate or –
- addresses *only* one part of the writing task.
- *may* provide a *weak, if any,* thesis; demonstrates *little* or ***no*** consistency of tone and focus; and illustrates *little* or ***no*** control of organization.
- *fails* to support ideas with details and/or examples.
- may provide ***no*** sentence variety and uses *limited* vocabulary.
- may demonstrate ***no*** sense of audience.
- may contain *serious errors* in the conventions of the English language. (Errors interfere with the reader's understanding of the essay.)*

A Persuasive Composition:
- *fails* to defend a position with any evidence and *fails* to address the reader's concerns, biases, and expectations.

non-scorable

B = Blank	**T** = Off-Topic
L = Written in a language other than English	**I** = Illegible / Unintelligible

* Conventions of the English language refer to grammar, punctuation, spelling, capitalization, and usage.

Note: Scoring Guides are reprinted, by permission, from *California High School Exit Exam (CAHSEE)*, California Department of Education, P.O. Box 271, Sacramento, CA 95812-0271.

CAHSEE
English-Language Arts

Answer Sheets

Answer Sheet

Practice Test 1

1. Ⓐ Ⓑ Ⓒ Ⓓ	25. Ⓐ Ⓑ Ⓒ Ⓓ	49. Ⓐ Ⓑ Ⓒ Ⓓ
2. Ⓐ Ⓑ Ⓒ Ⓓ	26. Ⓐ Ⓑ Ⓒ Ⓓ	50. Ⓐ Ⓑ Ⓒ Ⓓ
3. Ⓐ Ⓑ Ⓒ Ⓓ	27. Ⓐ Ⓑ Ⓒ Ⓓ	51. Ⓐ Ⓑ Ⓒ Ⓓ
4. Ⓐ Ⓑ Ⓒ Ⓓ	28. Ⓐ Ⓑ Ⓒ Ⓓ	52. Ⓐ Ⓑ Ⓒ Ⓓ
5. Ⓐ Ⓑ Ⓒ Ⓓ	29. Ⓐ Ⓑ Ⓒ Ⓓ	53. Ⓐ Ⓑ Ⓒ Ⓓ
6. Ⓐ Ⓑ Ⓒ Ⓓ	30. Ⓐ Ⓑ Ⓒ Ⓓ	54. Ⓐ Ⓑ Ⓒ Ⓓ
7. Ⓐ Ⓑ Ⓒ Ⓓ	31. Ⓐ Ⓑ Ⓒ Ⓓ	55. Ⓐ Ⓑ Ⓒ Ⓓ
8. Ⓐ Ⓑ Ⓒ Ⓓ	32. Ⓐ Ⓑ Ⓒ Ⓓ	56. Ⓐ Ⓑ Ⓒ Ⓓ
9. Ⓐ Ⓑ Ⓒ Ⓓ	33. Ⓐ Ⓑ Ⓒ Ⓓ	57. Ⓐ Ⓑ Ⓒ Ⓓ
10. Ⓐ Ⓑ Ⓒ Ⓓ	34. Ⓐ Ⓑ Ⓒ Ⓓ	58. Ⓐ Ⓑ Ⓒ Ⓓ
11. Ⓐ Ⓑ Ⓒ Ⓓ	35. Ⓐ Ⓑ Ⓒ Ⓓ	59. Ⓐ Ⓑ Ⓒ Ⓓ
12. Ⓐ Ⓑ Ⓒ Ⓓ	36. Ⓐ Ⓑ Ⓒ Ⓓ	60. Ⓐ Ⓑ Ⓒ Ⓓ
13. Ⓐ Ⓑ Ⓒ Ⓓ	37. Ⓐ Ⓑ Ⓒ Ⓓ	61. Ⓐ Ⓑ Ⓒ Ⓓ
14. Ⓐ Ⓑ Ⓒ Ⓓ	38. Ⓐ Ⓑ Ⓒ Ⓓ	62. Ⓐ Ⓑ Ⓒ Ⓓ
15. Ⓐ Ⓑ Ⓒ Ⓓ	39. Ⓐ Ⓑ Ⓒ Ⓓ	63. Ⓐ Ⓑ Ⓒ Ⓓ
16. Ⓐ Ⓑ Ⓒ Ⓓ	40. Ⓐ Ⓑ Ⓒ Ⓓ	64. Ⓐ Ⓑ Ⓒ Ⓓ
17. Ⓐ Ⓑ Ⓒ Ⓓ	41. Ⓐ Ⓑ Ⓒ Ⓓ	65. Ⓐ Ⓑ Ⓒ Ⓓ
18. Ⓐ Ⓑ Ⓒ Ⓓ	42. Ⓐ Ⓑ Ⓒ Ⓓ	66. Ⓐ Ⓑ Ⓒ Ⓓ
19. Ⓐ Ⓑ Ⓒ Ⓓ	43. Ⓐ Ⓑ Ⓒ Ⓓ	67. Ⓐ Ⓑ Ⓒ Ⓓ
20. Ⓐ Ⓑ Ⓒ Ⓓ	44. Ⓐ Ⓑ Ⓒ Ⓓ	68. Ⓐ Ⓑ Ⓒ Ⓓ
21. Ⓐ Ⓑ Ⓒ Ⓓ	45. Ⓐ Ⓑ Ⓒ Ⓓ	69. Ⓐ Ⓑ Ⓒ Ⓓ
22. Ⓐ Ⓑ Ⓒ Ⓓ	46. Ⓐ Ⓑ Ⓒ Ⓓ	70. Ⓐ Ⓑ Ⓒ Ⓓ
23. Ⓐ Ⓑ Ⓒ Ⓓ	47. Ⓐ Ⓑ Ⓒ Ⓓ	71. Ⓐ Ⓑ Ⓒ Ⓓ
24. Ⓐ Ⓑ Ⓒ Ⓓ	48. Ⓐ Ⓑ Ⓒ Ⓓ	72. Ⓐ Ⓑ Ⓒ Ⓓ

Writing Task

Writing Task

Writing Task

Writing Task

Answer Sheet

Practice Test 2

1. Ⓐ Ⓑ Ⓒ Ⓓ	25. Ⓐ Ⓑ Ⓒ Ⓓ	49. Ⓐ Ⓑ Ⓒ Ⓓ
2. Ⓐ Ⓑ Ⓒ Ⓓ	26. Ⓐ Ⓑ Ⓒ Ⓓ	50. Ⓐ Ⓑ Ⓒ Ⓓ
3. Ⓐ Ⓑ Ⓒ Ⓓ	27. Ⓐ Ⓑ Ⓒ Ⓓ	51. Ⓐ Ⓑ Ⓒ Ⓓ
4. Ⓐ Ⓑ Ⓒ Ⓓ	28. Ⓐ Ⓑ Ⓒ Ⓓ	52. Ⓐ Ⓑ Ⓒ Ⓓ
5. Ⓐ Ⓑ Ⓒ Ⓓ	29. Ⓐ Ⓑ Ⓒ Ⓓ	53. Ⓐ Ⓑ Ⓒ Ⓓ
6. Ⓐ Ⓑ Ⓒ Ⓓ	30. Ⓐ Ⓑ Ⓒ Ⓓ	54. Ⓐ Ⓑ Ⓒ Ⓓ
7. Ⓐ Ⓑ Ⓒ Ⓓ	31. Ⓐ Ⓑ Ⓒ Ⓓ	55. Ⓐ Ⓑ Ⓒ Ⓓ
8. Ⓐ Ⓑ Ⓒ Ⓓ	32. Ⓐ Ⓑ Ⓒ Ⓓ	56. Ⓐ Ⓑ Ⓒ Ⓓ
9. Ⓐ Ⓑ Ⓒ Ⓓ	33. Ⓐ Ⓑ Ⓒ Ⓓ	57. Ⓐ Ⓑ Ⓒ Ⓓ
10. Ⓐ Ⓑ Ⓒ Ⓓ	34. Ⓐ Ⓑ Ⓒ Ⓓ	58. Ⓐ Ⓑ Ⓒ Ⓓ
11. Ⓐ Ⓑ Ⓒ Ⓓ	35. Ⓐ Ⓑ Ⓒ Ⓓ	59. Ⓐ Ⓑ Ⓒ Ⓓ
12. Ⓐ Ⓑ Ⓒ Ⓓ	36. Ⓐ Ⓑ Ⓒ Ⓓ	60. Ⓐ Ⓑ Ⓒ Ⓓ
13. Ⓐ Ⓑ Ⓒ Ⓓ	37. Ⓐ Ⓑ Ⓒ Ⓓ	61. Ⓐ Ⓑ Ⓒ Ⓓ
14. Ⓐ Ⓑ Ⓒ Ⓓ	38. Ⓐ Ⓑ Ⓒ Ⓓ	62. Ⓐ Ⓑ Ⓒ Ⓓ
15. Ⓐ Ⓑ Ⓒ Ⓓ	39. Ⓐ Ⓑ Ⓒ Ⓓ	63. Ⓐ Ⓑ Ⓒ Ⓓ
16. Ⓐ Ⓑ Ⓒ Ⓓ	40. Ⓐ Ⓑ Ⓒ Ⓓ	64. Ⓐ Ⓑ Ⓒ Ⓓ
17. Ⓐ Ⓑ Ⓒ Ⓓ	41. Ⓐ Ⓑ Ⓒ Ⓓ	65. Ⓐ Ⓑ Ⓒ Ⓓ
18. Ⓐ Ⓑ Ⓒ Ⓓ	42. Ⓐ Ⓑ Ⓒ Ⓓ	66. Ⓐ Ⓑ Ⓒ Ⓓ
19. Ⓐ Ⓑ Ⓒ Ⓓ	43. Ⓐ Ⓑ Ⓒ Ⓓ	67. Ⓐ Ⓑ Ⓒ Ⓓ
20. Ⓐ Ⓑ Ⓒ Ⓓ	44. Ⓐ Ⓑ Ⓒ Ⓓ	68. Ⓐ Ⓑ Ⓒ Ⓓ
21. Ⓐ Ⓑ Ⓒ Ⓓ	45. Ⓐ Ⓑ Ⓒ Ⓓ	69. Ⓐ Ⓑ Ⓒ Ⓓ
22. Ⓐ Ⓑ Ⓒ Ⓓ	46. Ⓐ Ⓑ Ⓒ Ⓓ	70. Ⓐ Ⓑ Ⓒ Ⓓ
23. Ⓐ Ⓑ Ⓒ Ⓓ	47. Ⓐ Ⓑ Ⓒ Ⓓ	71. Ⓐ Ⓑ Ⓒ Ⓓ
24. Ⓐ Ⓑ Ⓒ Ⓓ	48. Ⓐ Ⓑ Ⓒ Ⓓ	72. Ⓐ Ⓑ Ⓒ Ⓓ

Writing Task

Writing Task

Writing Task

Writing Task

CAHSEE
English-Language Arts

Index

Index